Country Star TRACY BYRD Uses Rubs & Marinades To Create Memorable Meals

Compiled by Craig Lamb

[interactive blvd.]™

An Interactive Blvd.™ Book

www.InteractiveBlvd.com

Published by Interactive Blvd.™, a Division of 4964 Productions, LLC,
121 21st Ave. North, Suite 305, Nashville, Tennessee 37203.

Design by Creative Access, Inc., Nashville, Tennessee
Introduction photo courtesy Russ Harrington
Bus photo by Glenn Rose
Other photography by Ed Rode
Recipe and Copy Contributors: John Gallaspy and Craig Lamb

Library of Congress Control Number: 2003115059

Printed in the USA

* Table of Contents

Introduction

S ome of the simple things in life that should matter the most have been blown away by this whirlwind of a world in which we live. For kids, a mouse and computer game has taken the place of a ball, a bat and a game of backyard baseball. For grownups, sending an e-mail has taken the place of having a meaningful face-to-face conversation with a friend.

As a result of this fast pace of life, the fuel we put into our bodies has been reduced to whatever can be grabbed from the freezer, nuked in the microwave and then eaten in one hand on the go. Simply put, eating has taken the place of cooking real food.

Life in the Byrd house is like any other in America. In the morning we get up, grab what we can for breakfast, pack lunches and take my daughter Evee and son Logan to school with Jared, the newest Byrd, in tow. But after the pandemonium subsides, Michelle and I start thinking about what to cook for dinner. Remember that word: cook. It is a word that is becoming lost in the vocabulary of many Americans.

Cooking dinner used to be a big deal and, in our house, it still is. Every chance we have, and that means any time I am home from touring, Michelle and I like to make an event out of cooking dinner for our family and friends. For us, cooking together is one of the ways we bond and connect.

Cooking dinner is part of our family foundation. It should be for you, too, and especially when it comes down to the rare occasions most of us have time to spend in the kitchen with somebody special.

A frozen meal inside a box can't compare to the thought and preparation that goes into a full-blown, home cooked meal. When the food hits the table at the Byrd house we take life out of gear for a half-an-hour or more to talk about the events of the day. It is our time to bond with our kids and each other.

Michelle and I both grew up in small Texas towns where cooking still is part of everyday life. And that's why I recorded the song "Tiny Town" on my RCA release, *The Truth About Men*. One of my favorite verses in the song is "And we played in the street 'til my mom said come eat... In that tiny town."

If you come from a tiny town then you know exactly what I'm talking about. Some of us move away to big city jobs and that's part of life these days. But we take with us the memories of sitting down for a big spread of home cooked delicacies unlike anything you could order at any five-star restaurant.

Some of those precious memories are preserved in the form of index cards or scraps of paper with handwritten recipes from grandma's kitchen. And that is what this cookbook is all about. Hopefully, it will stir memories of life in a tiny town and inspire you to spend more time in the kitchen, stirring up a home cooked meal to share with family and friends. Enjoy.

Tracy Byrd

Rubs

Road Food

*R*oad Food... the very thought of it sends a warning to my stomach to get ready to be hit with a gastronomical shock. One meal might be a big beef burrito washed down with a frozen lime drink and the next might be a huge spread from a county fair. More on that one coming up...

But most of the time eating on the road is just that... eating. There is no cooking involved. Our tour bus has a microwave and fridge, but they rarely get used. Sometimes I remember to bring along leftovers from home to heat up for dinner, but that makes me even more homesick for a home cooked meal!

Before the bus exits the interstate on a long road trip I can spot the neon signs glowing along the roadside where we'll stop for a quick bite to eat at a fast food chain. Sometimes you are forced to get creative when the options can't satisfy your appetite. When that happens I go searching through the cabinets for anything that can be defined as edible. And what I come up with can sometimes bring a whole new meaning to the definition of Road Food!

Plastic is a word that is synonymous with Road Food. You go to a steak house and get a nice, juicy cut of prime rib to go and the order taker asks if you need plastic silverware. Everything comes wrapped in some form of plastic, regardless of how good it is or what it costs.

Don't get me wrong, not all Road Food is bad. It is always a good sign when the route to a show takes us way off the interstate and down a winding two-lane road. It is along these byways where some of the best Road Food is to be found. The Deep South and the rural Midwest are two of my favorite places to search out good Road Food. The best establishments are not even called restaurants. They are the classic BBQ joints and roadside diners where nothing has changed for years. The menu is the same because there has been no reason to change it. You can always identify one of the wannabes in this category of Road Food. The place is a fake if it serves sandwich "wraps" or more than one kind of coffee (black).

There is something to be said about pulling into a gravel parking lot where smoke is slowly drifting from a weathered barbecue pit tacked on to the backside of a dilapidated shack somewhere in the Mississippi Delta. The same old guy you saw stoking the pit on the last trip is still there. And he's been there for 30 years. Now that, my friends, is the essence of good Road Food.

These are places where a rub is something you put on food to make it taste better instead of what you massage into your skin to make it smoother.

I guess I should define what I mean when I say rub.

A rub is not a spice. Oregano is a spice. When you mix spices you get a rub.

Some folks call this mixture "seasoning." Where I come from, that's just another word for rub. They're one in the same.

There are a couple of rules about rubs I follow. Actually, they're sort of anti-rules.

One is you don't need to be exact when measuring them. If a recipe calls for one tablespoon of Smokin' Cajun Seasoning, just open the bottle and approximate. Heck, if you like your food hot keep pouring until you think it's enough to bring water to your eyes.

I even find myself improving on recipes this way. The last time I made my Blackened Catfish I added a little more of the Garlic Pepper Seasoning Mix than usual and it turned out even better! (Don't worry; the improved recipe is in the cookbook on page 140.)

The other anti-rule is that it's not a bad thing to mix, match and substitute. If you run out of one thing, just mix in something else, taste it, and if it works go for it. After all, a rub is a mixture of spices in the first place.

That's how we came up with the mixtures in my line of seasonings... by mixing and matching spices until we found the best pairings.

But having a great tasting rub is just the first part. What you do with the rub is just as important. You don't just sprinkle it on your food and toss it in the oven or on the grill.

Be sure to rub it into the food — the name "rub" is no coincidence. Make sure you get it into every nook and cranny. This gets the most flavor into the food. By doing this you ensure the flavors are absorbed throughout and you'll taste them in every bite, not just on the surface.

So grab a couple bottles of rubs and start having fun!

Marinades

The County Fair

$\mathcal{C}$ooking isn't the only part of Americana that is destined to someday become a chapter for a history book. The county fair is another fading and endangered tradition in this country. Fortunately, there are still some great county fairs out there and for that I am thankful for two reasons.

Number one, the fans that come see you at a county fair are some of the best. They are the true lovers of country music and have a very deep appreciation for the genre. Secondly, at county fairs cooking is a sport, a competition and a matter of personal pride. It is at the county fair in rural North Carolina where you can still find an Aunt Bee type who takes pride in taking home a blue ribbon for winning the baking contest with her homemade biscuits. It is at county fair in west Texas where the chili cook-off is won every year by the town sheriff. Or it's at a fair held in Iowa where the best cooks square off to create the best fried or creamed corn you've ever tasted.

Not surprisingly, the county fair is one of my favorite venues for playing a show. At the big shows we play the concert promoter gets a local caterer or restaurant to feed our band and crew before the show. To their credit, the food is not bad. But it's far from homemade.

When we play a county fair, the best cooks in the county turn out to make a gut-busting spread of home cooked food for the band and stage crew. To be chosen for the job is a status symbol where bragging rights run deep.

These are ladies who know how to cook and are what my song "Tiny Town" is all about. They spend all day long in the kitchen stirring, frying and simmering food that is cooked inside seasoned cast iron skillets handed down to them from their mothers. The recipes are valued heirlooms passed down through generations and the end result is nothing short of absolutely awesome.

It is a welcome sight to come off the stage at 5 o'clock after a pre-show sound check and find rows of tables, complete with red-and-white checked tablecloths, bulging with delicious fried chicken and vegetables that were hand picked that morning from a backyard garden.

What comes to mind when you think of a county fair? I think of a place where cooking and food is just as much a part of the event as the rides and the shows. From a turkey leg bought from a food vendor on the midway, to a pot luck dinner of homemade fried chicken, fresh vegetables and blue-ribbon desserts, you just can't beat a county fair.

The secret to many of those meals is the marinade. The meat on the grill at that rural Tennessee county fair may be the perfect cut, but it's the marinade it sat in overnight that gives it that perfect kick.

I love cooking with marinades. Sure, it takes longer to prepare than when you use a rub, but the deep flavor it provides is worth the wait.

A good rule of thumb when cooking with marinades is to be liberal with them. Make sure you have enough to thoroughly soak the meat or vegetables. If you have contact on only one side of the steak you've done only half the job.

There's really only one tool you need to buy for marinating: a box of heavy-duty zip-top plastic bags. As you'll read in my recipes, the easiest way to marinate is to place the food in the bag, pour in your marinade, press out all the air in the bag, seal it and toss it in the fridge.

While there are some recipes that call for letting the food marinate at room temperature, the majority tell you to simply put it in the refrigerator for a few hours or overnight. This gives ample time for the flavors to do their thing and soak into the food.

It also makes it easy to get part of your cooking out of the way early so all you have to do when you come home from work is fire-up the oven, pull out the marinated meat and start cooking.

There's also another way I use my marinades — for basting. That extra flavor that comes from basting Sweet Southern Dijon Marinade on game hens while they're grilling makes all the difference… and it keeps them moist and juicy. (Try it for yourself; the recipe's on page 82.)

The Basics

Homeade versus City Cooking

I have dined in some of the fanciest gourmet eateries in big cities from New York to San Francisco, and points in between. In the culinary world they are considered five-star restaurants and rightfully so since their service, presentation and the creativity of the menu is superior.

Some of these fine establishments tack the word "homemade" on to the names of some dishes like mashed potatoes. But their ingredients destroy the essence of this basic comfort food. My thought is always that they are trying to replicate something that can only be done at home.

By reading this book you obviously agree with me. Home cooking is not something done in a restaurant by a line cook getting paid by the hour to prepare food on a menu. It is not a job at all, but instead a labor of love.

Home cooking is done over a stove with a lot of steam and a lot of grease. And in the case of this cookbook, home cooking is also about a lot of smoke and fire coming from a grill.

Home cooking is also about throwing away the guilt associated with fat grams, carbohydrates and calories. A lot of city folk miss this point. Living healthy is important and I follow that lifestyle. But every now and then you need a break from that blandness. That makes it okay to sin every once in a while and savor the taste of a home cooked meal even as you feel the weight piling on with every delectable bite. Just be sure not to overdo it!

There is a passion and personality that goes into a home cooked meal that you cannot taste in a restaurant. Every homemade recipe has a story to be told. It might be about the first time you prepared the dish for a special date. Or it could be from a holiday where everyone raved about a new dish you prepared that has since become a family tradition at Thanksgiving or Christmas. It could even be the fried fish recipe that brings back memories of the first time you took your kids fishing. Regardless of what the recipe is, you have a great memory that makes preparing and eating that dish surpass anything you could order at the finest restaurant in New York or any other place.

And that my friends, is the difference between home cooking and city cooking. The recipes in this book are intended for home cooking. If you happen to find a knock-off dish at a restaurant then by all means avoid eating it—especially if you are a fan of home cooking. There is just nothing like it anywhere else except at home.

*T*here are a few basics every cook needs to know. Some are essential, others are helpful. These next few pages have some of both.

Measurement conversions fall into the essential category. Not knowing how many ounces are in a cup, or how many onions becomes one cup once chopped, can mean the difference between a tasty meal and one you end up giving to the dog.

Keep these charts near by and you'll never have the problem of putting too much of my Ultimate Seasoning on your chicken and spoiling a good home cooked meal. You can also visit www.EatLikeAByrd.com and download handy conversion charts to keep in the kitchen.

Conversion Charts

Dry

1/4 cup = 4 Tablespoons

1/3 cup = 5 Tablespoons + 1 teaspoon

1/2 cup = 8 Tablespoons or 4 oz.

3/4 cup = 12 Tablespoons

1 cup = 16 Tablespoons

1 cup = 48 teaspoons

2 cups = 1 pint

4 cups = 1 quart

1 oz. = 1/16 pound

2 oz. = 1/8 pound

3 oz. = 3/16 pound

4 oz. = 1/4 pound

8 oz. = 1/2 pound

12 oz. = 3/4 pound

16 oz. = 1 pound

32 oz. = 2 pounds

1 kilogram = 2.2 pounds or 35.2 oz.

Liquid

1/2 Tablespoon = 1 1/2 teaspoons

1 Tablespoon = 3 teaspoons

2 Tablespoon = 1 fluid ounce

1/4 cup = 2 fluid oz. or 4 Tablespoons

1/3 cup = 2 2/3 fluid oz. or 5 Tablespoons + 1 teaspoon

1/2 cup = 4 fluid oz. or 8 Tablespoons

2/3 cup = 5 1/3 fluid ounce or 10 Tablespoons + 2 teaspoons

3/4 cup = 6 fluid oz. or 12 Tablespoons

7/8 cup = 7 fluid oz. or 14 tablepsoons

1 cup = 8 fluid oz. or 16 Tablespoons

2 cups = 16 fluid oz. or 1 pint

2 pints = 32 fluid oz. or 1 quart

4 quarts = 1 gallon

Food

1 stick butter = 8 Tablespoons butter

1 pound butter = 4 sticks butter

1/2 pound hard cheese = approximately 2 cups grated cheese

1 pound apples = approximately 3 apples

1 medium lemon = approximately 3 Tablespoons lemon juice or 2 or 3 teaspoons grated peel

1 large onion = approximately 1 cup chopped onion

1 cup raw converted rice = 4 cups cooked rice

1 large tomato = approximately 3/4 cup chopped tomato

1 pound all-purpose flour = approximately 4 cups sifted flour

2 slices bread = 1 cup fresh breadcrumbs

Baking

1 cup sifted cake flour = 1 cup minus 2 Tablespoons sifted all purpose flour

1 cup sifted all purpose flour = 1 cup + 2 Tablespoons sifted cake flour

1 teaspoon double-acting baking powder = 1/4 teaspoon baking soda + 1/2 teaspoon cream of tartar

Miscellaneous

1 cup stock = 1 bouillon cube dissolved in 1 cup of boiling water

1 ounce unsweetened chocolate = 3 Tablespoons cocoa powder + 1 Tablespoon butter

1 ounce semisweet chocolate = 3 Tablespoons cocoa powder + 2 Tablespoons butter + 3 Tablespoons sugar

1 Tablespoon prepared mustard = 1 teaspoon dried mustard

On the helpful side...

Here are tips that have been handed down to me by my NaNa, aunts, mother and friends. Some of these you may know, others will be new to you, but they all can make cooking a bit simpler for you.

- Always preheat your oven and let it run through a cycle before putting your dish in. And don't keep opening the door to see if it's done; all that does is let hot air out and lower the oven temperature. Use your oven light or wait until you're pretty certain it's ready.

- To peel a tomato, drop it in a pot of boiling water for about 20 seconds and then put it under cold water. Then, with a sharp knife, cut two slits, crosswise, at the stem end and peel the skin away. It should come off easily; if it doesn't repeat the hot/cold process for about 10 seconds more and you should be in good shape.

- To get the best results, and greatest volume, when whipping egg whites let the egg whites warm to room temperature first.

- To peel a clove of garlic, simply place it on a flat surface and hit it with the flat edge of a chef's or other large knife and press down. That will loosen the "paper" casing and you can slide the clove right out.

- Before frying breaded foods, let them stand at room temperature for 20 minutes or so the coating will stick better.

- Before you start cooking, read the recipe all the way through so you know what comes when and how long each step takes. Then gather all of your ingredients and prep. This way you'll have what you need when you need it, and you won't run into any surprises.

- When measuring flour (or similar ingredients) always spoon the flour into the measuring cup. Don't use the measuring cup as a scoop; this packs the flour into the cup too much and you'll get more than you want.

- The only ingredient you ever want to pack when measuring is brown sugar.

- When measuring liquids always leave the measuring cup on the counter and bend down to see how much you've poured. When you bring the measuring cup up to eye level you'll end up holding it at an angle — no matter how hard you try — and you won't actually have the amount you think you have.

There's also a basic thing you need to know about this cookbook that will help you pick your menu... and which new recipes you want to try.

At the bottom of each page you'll find my Tiny Town logo — that's the illustration of me playing the guitar.

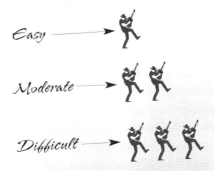

Easy ·········▶

Moderate ·········▶

Difficult ·········▶

If you see one logo, that's an easy recipe even the most novice cook can prepare like a chef. If you see three of me at the bottom you've found a difficult recipe that may take you more time to prepare. If there are two logos then the recipe falls somewhere in between. But don't let the harder recipes scare you away; part of the fun of cooking is trying new things and finding new favorite foods!

Tools You'll Need

NaNa's House

Everyone has a favorite grandma and mine was Mavis Vaughn, who I called NaNa ever since I learned to talk. She passed away in 2001, at the age of 73, after living a full and complete life and I sure do miss her.

NaNa was my best friend and the one who introduced me to the awesome world of the outdoors. I could literally write a book about the long days and nights we spent fishing, hunting, trapping and watching wildlife in the bayous, rivers and backcountry of southeast Texas.

Everything we ate at NaNa's came from the woods and waters or was home grown. I guess you could say that NaNa shopped at the original "organic" grocery store called the great outdoors. Together, we gathered fresh eggs for breakfast from the hen house and picked fresh tomatoes, okra, corn, peppers and other veggies to can and put up for the winter.

She even made her own beer in the barn, reasoning that the brew aging inside gallon milk jugs fermented better in the heat. Now, I wouldn't say NaNa made good beer, but I always admired her for making her own.

Like all grandmas, my NaNa was a great cook and she could flat throw it on the table when it came time to eat. Not surprisingly, the kitchen was the centerpiece of her big house. Out back was a garden so big that she worked it with a mule-drawn plow. On the front porch was a huge chest freezer packed with fish, venison and every other edible critter that flew, swam or crawled.

NaNa's kitchen was the busiest place in the house. Seasoned cast iron cookware of every shape and size was used to prepare breakfast, lunch and dinner. There was no microwave since the food was so good there were never any leftovers. It was all consumed in one, long sitting. There was always something simmering on the gas cook top or baking in the big oven. In the wintertime she didn't need to heat the kitchen because the warmth from the oven and stove kept the whole room toasty and filled with the delicious aroma of whatever she had cooking at the time.

NaNa's kitchen was always open to anyone. If something smelled good and you wanted a taste you could just dip a big spoon into the pot and sample what was simmering inside. That could have been anything from squirrel dumplings or pot roast, to fresh butter beans or fried corn.

These days, canning fresh vegetables and fruits or cooking a pot roast in a big dutch oven have been replaced by frozen foods and roasts that you bake in a bag. The kitchen at our house is a gourmet kitchen by anyone's standards; it has all the latest gadgets and non-stick cookware. But some things never change. Inside one of the drawers is a seasoned cast iron skillet and a dutch oven and every time I use them I can still smell the aroma of something that was cooked in them years ago in NaNa's kitchen.

A cast iron skillet, like the one from NaNa's kitchen, is one of those tools that's indispensable. You'll find yourself pulling it out for several recipes in this book.

There are some other tools you'll need to make the most of your cooking. They aren't fancy and don't have to be expensive, but you need them around.

In the pots and pans category you'll need a couple of sauce pans with covers. I find if you have a 1 1/2 quart and a 3 quart one in the cabinet you'll be able to handle most anything a recipe throws your way.

Same goes for skillets, although NaNa always called them frying pans. These are sloped edged pans, and you don't need a lid for these. You'll want at least two of them around — an 8" and a 12" one. It's always good to have at least one skillet be non-stick.

You'll also want to have a stock pot (8 quarts is a good size), a roasting pan and two or three mixing bowls.

And while it won't fit in your cabinet, you'll find a lot of recipes in this book call for a grill. It can be gas or charcoal, but there are few things that taste better than meals made over hot coals or a fire.

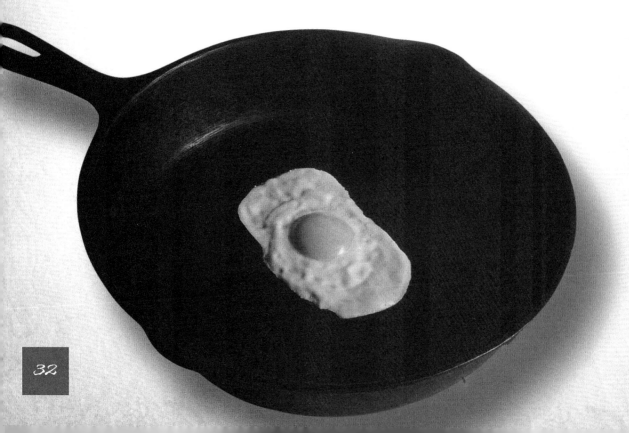

Other than that, some knives, spoons and cooking utensils will have you on your way. Well, almost.

One of NaNa's basic cooking lessons was the most important tools weren't made of metal or wood, and you didn't cook in them. You cooked with them.

Seasonings and spices are what make a good meal great. That's one reason why I created the Tiny Town line of seasonings and marinades based on the ones NaNa and others in my family used when I was growing up, and the ones I've tasted while performing on the road.

You'll also want some other basic spices and herbs around before you start cooking.

- basil
- bay leaf
- cayenne
- chili powder
- cinnamon
- cloves
- cumin
- curry powder
- dill weed
- garlic
- garlic powder

- ginger
- mustard
- nutmeg
- olive oil
- oregano
- paprika
- peppercorns
- rosemary
- salt
- soy sauce
- thyme

As you cook you'll find your own favorite tools, of course. But, if you have these in your kitchen you're ready to start eating like a Byrd.

Meats

Growing Up Outdoors with NaNa

The heritage of the great outdoors was passed down to me by NaNa, my special grandma who fished, trapped and hunted well into her 70s. That is amazing to me and I hope I can follow in her footsteps.

NaNa also taught me how to cook and about respecting the bounty of the great outdoors and not abusing it. And it is because of her that I enjoy the full outdoor experience, from the anticipation of the trip, to preparing a meal made of wild game and fish brought to the table by my hands.

I have many, many fond memories of the fishing and hunting trips we took over the years. One of the best was the first squirrel I took with the small gauge shotgun she gave me when I was only 10 years old. Another was the final time we went hunting, a story I will tell later in this book because it means so much to me.

A typical fall Saturday with NaNa began bright and early with the smell of bacon and fried potatoes wafting across the kitchen into my bedroom. If I close my eyes I can still smell the potatoes cooking and hear the crackle of the bacon in the cast iron skillet.

After a hearty breakfast, NaNa would fix our lunch, which consisted of scrambled egg and potted meat sandwiches. Then we'd slip quietly out the back door and hunt squirrels in the hardwood river bottom land behind her house. Eventually, we'd end up on the Neches River where she kept a little 12-foot aluminum johnboat tied to big cypress tree on the bank.

She'd start the 4 h.p. motor and we'd emerge from the dark bayou into the sunny river channel, its muddy water carving deep holes into the shoreline. It was in these deep, cool holes that we'd check her trot lines which were baited with the most awful smelling bait. It was her homemade concoction and man, it sure caught the catfish.

Running the trot lines took until lunch time when we ate what I called "NaNa's All-Day Sandwiches," because they'd control your appetite until dinner. Depending on our luck we either went bass fishing during the afternoon or headed back to the house with the catch. After she cleaned the fish they went into gallon milk jugs cut off at the handle. I'd fill them up with water, put them into the deep freeze and they'd be preserved for months.

No matter what the season NaNa always had something going outdoors. Sometimes we didn't carry a shotgun or fishing pole. Sometimes we took along a pair of binoculars and a sense of adventure and went wildlife viewing.

I feel fortunate to have been exposed to my grandma's deep love and respect of the outdoors. The legacy of fishing and hunting passed on to me by NaNa makes me more passionate about clean air and water. I want it for my kids and so should you.

Tracy's Smokin' Cajun Meat Loaf

2 teaspoons olive oil

1 cup onion, finely chopped

1/4 cup celery, finely chopped

1/2 cup green bell pepper, finely chopped

2 garlic cloves, minced

2 eggs

1/2 cup bread crumbs

1/2 cup barbeque sauce, divided

1/4 cup parsley, finely chopped

1 teaspoon Tracy's Smokin' Cajun Seasoning

1 Tablespoon Worcestershire

3/4 teaspoon salt

1 1/2 pounds ground chuck

1 pound ground pork

4 oz. smoked sausage, diced

Preheat oven to 350°.

Heat oil in a skillet over medium heat. Add onion, celery, bell pepper and garlic and cook until soft, about 4 to 5 minutes. Place in a bowl and set aside until it reaches room temperature.

Wisk eggs into the onion mixture; stir in the bread crumbs, 1/4 cup barbeque sauce, parsley, Tracy's Smokin' Cajun Seasoning, Worcestershire and salt. Stir well. Then add the beef and pork and mix thoroughly (using your hands is the best way, even if it is a bit messy). Shape the meat mixture into a loaf and place in a loaf or baking pan.

Bake at 350° for 30 minutes, then baste the meatloaf with more of the barbeque sauce and bake for another 15 minutes. Baste again with the remaining barbeque sauce and bake for another 15 minutes or until done. Remove and let sit 10 to 15 minutes before serving.

Prep time: 30 minutes • Cook Time: 1 hour • Serves: 8

Beef Stir Fry

2 pounds of thinly sliced steak

1 Tablespoon salt

1/2 Tablespoon black pepper

1/4 cup lime juice

1 Tablespoon sugar

1/4 cup white wine

2 Tablespoons Tracy's Sweet & Tangy Marinade

1 Tablespoon ginger, chopped

1 clove garlic, minced

2 Tablespoons oil

1 carrot, cut in fine strips lengthwise

1 red bell pepper, cut in little finger sized strips lengthwise

2 green onions, cut in long strips

1 Tablespoon cornstarch

1 cup water

Cooked white or wild rice

Salt and pepper the meat. Combine the lime juice, sugar, white wine, Tracy's Sweet & Tangy Marinade, ginger and garlic in a bowl and set aside. In a large iron skillet or wok heat the oil and brown the meat for about 4 to 5 minutes. Add the vegetables and stir for another 2 to 3 minutes. Then, add the lime juice mixture and stir until it boils. Mix the cornstarch and water and add it to the skillet, stirring constantly, and let it boil again. Serve over the rice.

Prep time: 35 minutes • Cook Time: 20 minutes • Serves: 6 to 8

Beef Cabbage Rolls

1 medium head of cabbage

Water

Salt

1 egg

1 pound ground beef

3 Tablespoons celery, chopped

3/4 cup cooked white rice

1/2 cup onion, chopped

1/4 teaspoon cinnamon

1/4 teaspoon Tabasco®

1 Tablespoon Tracy's Ultimate Seasoning

1 can (8oz.) tomato sauce

3 Tablespoons green pepper, chopped

2 cans (10 1/2 oz.) tomato soup

1 Tablespoon dried parsley

Preheat the oven to 350°.

Wash, trim and core the cabbage. Place the cabbage bottom down in a saucepan with 4 inches of boiling salt water. Cover and simmer for 4 minutes or until the leaves are soft. Drain and let cool so you can separate the leaves from the cabbage head. Pat fairly dry.

Whip the egg and combine with all the other ingredients, except the tomato soup and parsley, and mix thoroughly. Divide the mixture into 12 equal parts and roll each within a cabbage leaf, securing with a wooden toothpick. Place the finished rolls in a baking dish with the seam side down. Next, mix the tomato soup with about 6 oz. of water and parsley flakes and pour this over the cabbage rolls. Cover and bake at 350° degrees for an hour. Remove the lid and turn on broil for about 5 minutes to give it a little texture.

Prep time: 30 minutes • Cook time: 1 1/2 hours • Serves: 4

One Pan Spaghetti

1 pound ground sirloin

1 1/2 cups water

2 teaspoons chili powder

1 can (6 oz.) tomato paste

1 can (8 oz.) tomato sauce

1 pint tomato juice

1/8 teaspoon Tabasco®

1 cup onion, chopped

2 cloves of garlic, minced

2 teaspoons Tracy's Ultimate Seasoning

1 teaspoon salt

1/2 teaspoon pepper

1 teaspoon sugar

1 teaspoon oregano

Spaghetti (8 oz.)

Combine all the ingredients except the spaghetti in a large skillet, cover and bring to a boil. Reduce to a simmer and cook for 30 minutes. Add uncooked spaghetti. Stir to separate spaghetti strands, bring back to a boil and simmer until spaghetti is done, approximately 10 minutes.

Prep time: 10 minutes • Cook Time: 45 minutes • Serves: 4

Burgers on the Grill

2 pounds ground beef

1 cup white onion, finely chopped

1/2 cup green pepper, finely chopped

Salt & pepper

1 Tablespoon Tracy's Mesquite Grill Seasoning

3 Tablespoons Tracy's Sweet & Tangy Marinade

Mix all ingredients together well in a large bowl. Shape into 8 patties and refrigerate for at least an hour. Remove and grill on medium heat, turning twice until done.

Prep time: 15 minutes • Refrigerate: 1 hour • Cook time: 10 minutes • Serves: 8

Stuffed Bell Peppers

6 large bell peppers

Water

3 slices thick bacon

1 pound ground beef

1 medium onion, chopped

1/4 teaspoon dried oregano

1/2 teaspoon Tracy's Smokin' Cajun Seasoning

3/4 cup cooked rice

1/4 teaspoon dried thyme

1/4 teaspoon dried sweet basil

1 can (8oz.) tomato sauce

Dash Tabasco®

1/2 cup Parmesan cheese

Preheat oven to 350°.

Remove tops and seeds from bell peppers and discard. Place the seeded peppers in a large saucepan with enough water to cover. Bring to a boil and cook for about 4 to 5 minutes. Remove and drain.

Dice the bacon strips, place in a skillet and add the ground beef and onion. Sauté until brown. Add remaining ingredients (except cheese) and cook for about 5 minutes. Use this mixture to stuff the peppers. Place in a baking dish and bake at 350° for 1 hour. Remove and sprinkle with Parmesan cheese. Continue baking for about 10 to 15 minutes more or until cheese is melted.

Prep time: 30 minutes   •   Cook Time: 1 1/2 hours   •   Serves: 6

Steak and Bean Stew

2 pounds steak, cut into 1 inch cubes

1 pound dry lima beans

Tracy's Flame Kist Steak Seasoning

1/4 teaspoon celery salt

1 medium onion, chopped

1 Tablespoon Worcestershire

Soak beans overnight. Drain and place in heavy pot. Season the steak to taste with Tracy's Flame Kist Steak Seasoning and place in the pot. Add the remaining ingredients and cover with water. Simmer on low heat for 2 1/2 hours.

Prep time: 10 minutes • Soak beans: overnight • Cook time: 2 1/2 hours • Serves: 6 to 8

Bubba Burgers

2 pounds ground beef

2 Tablespoons Tracy's Mesquite Grill Seasoning

1 package cheese slices

1 large onion, thinly sliced

2 tomatoes, thinly sliced

Salt & pepper

Mix the ground beef with Tracy's Mesquite Grill Seasoning and shape into 8 patties - thinner, but larger, than usual. On top of four patties, place a layer of cheese, onion and tomato. Cover with the other patties and seal edges. Season with salt and pepper to taste. Grill over low heat until done (probably a little longer than usual burgers, or about 20 to 25 minutes), turning regularly.

Prep time: 25 minutes   •   Cook Time: 20 to 25 minutes   •   Serves: 4

South of the Border Steak Dinner

3 pounds beef, cubed

1/2 pound bacon, diced

1 medium onion, chopped

1 Tablespoon Tracy's Smokin' Cajun Seasoning

1 can (4 oz.) chopped chilies

Dash of Tabasco®

1 Tablespoon cumin

1 teaspoon oregano

1 quart water

1 can beer

1/2 cup yellow corn meal

16 oz. cooked pinto beans

8 flour tortillas

8 pickled jalapenos, whole

Sauté the beef cubes, bacon pieces and chopped onion, sprinkled with Tracy's Smokin' Cajun Seasoning, in an iron skillet until the beef is brown. Put this in a large pot and add the chilies, Tabasco®, cumin, oregano, water and beer. Simmer, covered, for 3 hours.

Skim off fat from bacon. Stir in yellow cornmeal and cook for another 5 minutes. Serve with the pinto beans, tortillas and peppers.

Prep time: 20 minutes • Cook time: 4 hours • Serves: 6

NaNa's Lasagna

2 pounds ground sirloin

2 Tablespoons parsley flakes

1 clove garlic, minced

1 Tablespoon basil

2 Tablespoons oregano

1 Tablespoon sugar

2 1/2 teaspoons salt

1 teaspoon rosemary

24 oz. crushed tomatoes

2 cans (6 oz.) tomato paste

1 package (10 oz.) lasagna noodles

3 cups cream style cottage cheese

2 eggs, beaten

1/2 cup Parmesan cheese, grated

1 pound Mozzarella cheese

Preheat the oven to 375°.

Brown the meat in a skillet and add the spices, tomatoes and tomato paste. Simmer 30 minutes. Cook noodles in boiling salted water until tender; drain and rinse in cold water. Combine cottage cheese, eggs and Parmesean cheese.

Place half the noodles in a 9x13" baking dish. Spread half the cottage cheese mixture over noodles, then spread half the Mozzarella cheese and then half the meat sauce. Repeat layers, saving a little of the Mozzarella. Top with the remaining Mozzarella. Bake at 375° for 30 minutes. Cool slightly.

Prep time: 35 to 40 minutes • Cook time: 1 hour 20 minutes • Serves: 4 to 6

Seasoned Tenderloin Appetizers

1 5-pound tenderloin

3 Tablespoons olive oil

2 Tablespoons Worcestershire

1/2 cup red wine

Dash Tobasco®

1 teaspoon thyme

1/2 teaspoon cumin

1/2 teaspoon oregano

1/8 teaspoon cloves

1/8 teaspoon garlic powder

1 teaspoon onion salt

Combine all ingredients. Pour over the tenderloin and refrigerate in a glass container for 6 to 8 hours, turning several times. Remove, reserving the marinade.

Preheat oven to 425°.

Using a meat thermometer, bake at 425° until the center reaches 160°, basting regularly with the marinade.

Allow the tenderloin to stand for about 10 minutes and cool slightly, to make slicing easier. Slice thinly and serve as an appetizer with rolls.

Prep time: 10 minutes • Marinate: 6 to 8 hours • Cook Time: 30 to 40 minutes • Serves: 8

Tracy's Best Brisket

5 to 6 pounds beef brisket

1/2 cup water

1/4 cup ketchup

1/4 cup light brown sugar

1 Tablespoon Worcestershire

1 teaspoon black pepper

1/2 teaspoon onion powder

1/4 cup apple cider vinegar

1/4 cup lemon juice

1 teaspoon dry mustard

1 teaspoon salt

1/2 teaspoon red pepper

1 teaspoon garlic powder

Combine all the ingredients and mix well. Pour over the brisket in a roasting pan and marinate, covered, in the refrigerator overnight.

Preheat oven to 225°.

Roast at 225° for about 4 to 5 hours.

Prep time: 20 minutes • Marinate: overnight • Cook time: 4 to 5 hours • Serves: 8 to 10

Baked Round Steak

2 to 3 pounds round steak, 1 inch thick

1/2 cup all purpose flour

2 teaspoons salt

1/4 teaspoon pepper

1 to 2 Tablespoons butter or margarine

2 to 3 Tablespoons olive or vegetable oil

3 Tablespoons onion, finely chopped

Brown sugar

Ketchup

Dried Basil leaves

1 Tablespoon butter

1/4 cup beef broth or bouillon broth

Preheat oven to 350°.

Trim meat and cut into serving size pieces. Pound to 1/2" thickness with a meat mallet. On a sheet of wax paper mix flour, salt and pepper. Dip steaks in flour mixture and turn to coat.

In a large skillet, melt 1 Tablespoon butter and 2 Tablespoons oil over a medium high heat. Add coated steaks; and brown on both sides. Fry in two batches if necessary, adding additional butter and oil. Arrange browned steaks in a 12 x 8" baking pan. Sprinkle the tops of the steaks with finely chopped onions.

Combine the brown sugar and ketchup until it has a thick paste-like consistency. Brush over the tops of the steak pieces. Sprinkle lightly with basil and dot with 1 Tablespoon butter. Add stock or bouillon to drippings in skillet and cook over medium heat for about 1 minute, stirring to loosen any browned bits. Pour this into baking pan. Cover with foil and bake for about 45 minutes. Remove foil. If meat appears dry, add a small amount of stock or water to pan. Bake until browned on top, about 15 minutes longer.

Prep time: 45 minutes   •   Cook Time: 1 1/2 hours   •   Serves: 6 to 8

Steak Jalapeno

1 2-pound steak

3 or 4 jalapeno peppers, fresh or pickled

1 Tablespoon salt

1/4 cup lime juice

1/2 cup olive oil

4 garlic cloves

1/2 Tablespoon ground black pepper

1 Tablespoon dried oregano

2 teaspoons Tracy's Flame Kist Steak Seasoning

Combine all the ingredients, except steak, in a blender and puree. Pour mixture over the steak in a shallow glass or ceramic dish and rub all over. Cover and marinate in the refrigerator for a day.

Remove and grill over medium heat about 10 minutes (for medium rare), turning once. Cut in thin slices across the grain and serve.

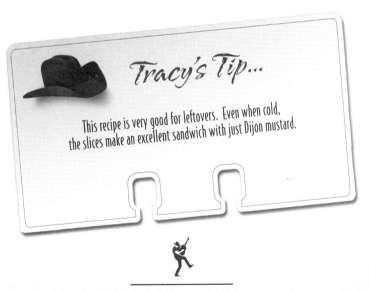

Tracy's Tip...

This recipe is very good for leftovers. Even when cold, the slices make an excellent sandwich with just Dijon mustard.

Prep time: 10 minutes • Marinate: overnight • Cook time: 10 to 15 minutes • Serves: 6 to 8

Pepper Steak

1 pound round steak
Tracy's Ultimate Seasoning, to taste
2 Tablespoons vegetable oil
1/4 cup onion, chopped
1 clove garlic, minced
1 bell pepper, cut into thin strips
1 teaspoon salt
Pepper
1 cube beef bouillon
1 cup hot water
2 Tablespoons Tracy's Sweet & Tangy Marinade
2 Tablespoons cornstarch
1/4 cup cold water
1 pound tomatoes, chopped (optional)

Cut steak in bite-size pieces, season to taste with Tracy's Ultimate Seasoning and brown in vegetable oil. Add the onion, garlic and bell pepper. Season with the salt and pepper. Dissolve the bouillon cube in the hot water and add to meat. Cover and simmer until the meat is tender, 20 to 25 minutes.

Combine Tracy's Sweet & Tangy Marinade, cornstarch and cold water and stir into the meat mixture. Simmer until the gravy thickens.

One pound of tomatoes can be added at the same time as the cornstarch mixture.

Tracy's Tip...

This is tasty served over mashed potatoes with some homemade biscuits.

Prep time: 20 minutes • Cook Time: 45 minutes • Serves: 4

Chicken Fried Steak

2 pounds steak (approximately 4 steaks)

1 egg, beaten

Salt & pepper to taste

1 teaspoon of Tracy's Ultimate Seasoning

1/2 cup all purpose flour

Vegetable oil

Dip each steak in beaten egg, then a mixture of salt, pepper, Tracy's Ultimate Seasoning and flour. Fry each steak in vegetable oil until browned.

Prep time: 10 minutes • Cook time: 20 minutes • Serves: 4

Tracy's Meatballs in Red Sauce

For the meatballs:

2 pounds ground sirloin

3/4 cup bread crumbs

2 eggs, beaten

1/4 cup fresh parsley, chopped

9 cloves garlic

1 teaspoon salt

4 oz. Romano, grated

2 Tablespoons olive oil, for frying

For the sauce:

3 cans (12 oz.) tomato paste

4 cups water

4 oz. Romano, grated

Mix bread crumbs and eggs. Add remaining ingredients (except oil) and form into 1 inch balls. Brown in a skillet with oil. Remove meatballs.

To make the sauce, add tomato paste to skillet with meatball drippings. Add 1 1/2 cups of water and cook until it bubbles. Add remaining water and bring to boil. Reduce heat and simmer, covered, for 30 minutes.

Add meatballs and simmer, covered, for 1 hour. Add the Romano right before serving. Serve over your favorite pasta with additional Romano for sprinkling.

Prep time: 30 minutes • Cook Time: 2 hours • Serves: 6 to 8

Ozark Beef Stew

2 pounds trimmed and cubed beef
1 cup flour
3 Tablespoons bacon drippings
1 can beer
1 1/2 cups red wine
2 Tablespoons Worcestershire
1 Tablespoon mixed herbs of your taste
1 Tablespoon parsley
1 teaspoon pepper
1 teaspoon Tracy's Ultimate Seasoning
1 green pepper, chopped
4 carrots, sliced 1/4" thick
2 Idaho or new potatoes, cubed
1 can (10 oz.) corn
1 large red onion, chopped
1 can (10 oz.) spicy stewed tomatoes, drained
1/2 cup lemon juice

Roll meat in flour, brown in skillet with bacon drippings. Transfer to pot and add beer, wine, Worcestershire, herbs, parsley, pepper, Tracy's Ultimate Seasoning and green pepper. Boil for 10 minutes, reducing heat to simmer for 2 to 3 hours, until meat is tender.

Add carrots, potatoes, corn, onion, stewed tomatoes and lemon juice. Let simmer for one hour or until vegetables are tender. Add more beer, water, or seasoning if needed. Serve hot!

Tracy's Tip...

If any of your stews are too salty, add several slices of raw potato and let it boil five minutes or so. Then take them out and you'll take out much of the salt, too.

Prep time: 30 minutes • Cook time: 4 to 4 1/2 hours • Serves: 6 to 8

Grilled Beef Kabobs and Vegetables

2 pounds cubed beef tenderloin

6 bell peppers, quatered

6 white onions, cut into chunks

1 pound fresh mushrooms, whole

6 firm tomatoes, quartered

For the marinade:

1 2/3 cup red wine vinegar

1 1/4 cup ketchup

3/4 cup olive oil

3/4 cup soy sauce

1/2 cup Tracy's Sweet & Tangy Marinade

2 Tablespoons prepared mustard

1 Tablespoon salt

1 Tablespoon pepper

1 Tablespoon Tracy's Garlic Pepper Seasoning

Mix the marinade and add cubed tenderloin, bell peppers and onions in a covered dish. Refrigerate overnight.

The next morning, add mushrooms and tomatoes and replace in the refrigerator until ready to cook.

Skewer on metal grill skewers and grill slowly low heat, basting with remaining sauce while cooking. Serve on skewers on platter.

Prep time: 20 minutes   •   Marinate: overnitght   •   Cook time: 15 to 20 minutes   •   Serves: 4 to 5

Jesse James Jerky

2 pounds round or flank steak, sliced 1/8" thick with grain

For the marinade:

2 Tablespoons Worcestershire

2 Tablespoons Tracy's Sweet & Tangy Marinade

2 cloves garlic, minced

1 Tablespoon salt

1 teaspoon ground red pepper

1 cup corn whiskey

1 cup water

Mix marinade ingredients and marinate meat strips in covered glass container overnight. Pat dry and place strips on racks so they do not touch.

Preheat oven to 150°.

In oven, cook at 150° for 6 hours with oven door slightly open.

Tracy's Tip...

For best results, cook in electric smoker for 12 hours outdoors (cooking time will vary depending upon outside temperature) using one pan or layer of wood chips only.

Prep time: 30 minutes • Refrigerate: overnight • Cook Time: 6 to 12 hours • Serves: 4

What Matters Most

$\mathcal{E}$veryone can probably relate to this Christmas story. You filled out your wish list, gave it to Santa Claus or a loved one and on Christmas morning you got everything but the one gift you wanted the most.

That happened to me one Christmas when I was entering my teenage years. It was a tradition for me to spend my Christmas vacation with my grandmother, NaNa. Every day, from sunup to sundown, we went stalking through the woods and bayous hunting everything from rabbit and deer, to quail and squirrel. And every Christmas vacation since I was six years old I hunted with the .410 gauge shotgun she gave me.

To me, my rites of passage as a teenager including moving up to a .12 gauge shotgun like the grownups used, NaNa included. It was no surprise to anyone when a Savage single shot .12 gauge shotgun appeared at the top of my Christmas wish list.

As you can imagine, my excitement grew with every passing day leading up to Christmas. Every morning I picked up that little .410 shotgun I knew that its days were numbered.

The big day finally arrived when NaNa took me home to spend Christmas Eve with my parents. I bolted through the front door and was blinded by the popping flash bulbs of my dad's camera as he snapped off pictures of me all wide eyed and grinning from ear-to-ear as I made a dash for the Christmas tree.

There were gifts everywhere. I searched through the pile only to find nothing resembling a shotgun. Instead there was a weight bench. At the time I played sports and my parents thought hitting the weights would help me put some muscles on my skinny frame.

The disappointment showed in my face and my dad remembered my first wish. He put his arm around my shoulder and told me we'd go and get my prized shotgun. We arrived at Gibson's Discount Center just as it was closing and went home with a colorful box containing my brand new shotgun. I was the luckiest kid on earth, or so I thought.

A few years later our house was vandalized and the loot included my most prized possession. Ironically, the weight bench was spared. I was crushed.

As I look back on that stage of my life I realize today what matters the most at Christmas. It's not about fretting over the gift I wanted and didn't find beneath the Christmas tree. Instead, it's all about giving thanks for the spiritual gifts that I am already blessed to have, among them my wife Michelle and our kids Evee, Logan and Jared... and a long, long list of friends and other blessings that don't come wrapped up in a box.

* Bourbon Glazed Ham

1 (6- to 8-pound) smoked ham half
1 cup honey
1/2 cup molasses
1/2 cup bourbon
1/4 cup orange juice
2 Tablespoons Tracy's Sweet Southern Dijon Marinade
2 teaspoons Dijon mustard

Preheat oven to 325°.

Heat honey and molasses in a saucepan over medium-high heat, whisking to blend. Remove from heat and whisk in bourbon, orange juice, Tracy's Sweet Southern Dijon Marinade and mustard.

Remove skin and excess fat from ham, and place ham in a roasting pan.

Bake at 325° on lower oven rack for 1 1/2 hours or until a meat thermometer inserted into thickest portion registers 140°. Baste ham periodically with honey mixture throughout the baking time.

Let ham stand for 15 minutes before slicing. While ham stands, bring drippings and remaining glaze to a boil in a small saucepan. Remove from heat. Serve glaze with sliced ham.

Prep time: 10 minutes • Cook time: 1 1/2 hours • Serves: 12 to 14

Caleb's Crockpot Stew

2 pounds beef, cubed

1 cup all purpose flour

Salt & pepper to taste

1 cup vegetable oil

3 ground beef patties

1 can (14 oz.) beef stew

3 potatoes, diced

1 package green onion soup mix

1 can 7-Up®

1 can cream of mushroom soup

1 onion, diced

Roll beef cubes in flour seasoned with salt & pepper. Heat vegetable oil in frying pan and brown beef cubes and hamburger patties. Combine browned beef and crumbled hamburger patties with other ingredients and place in a crockpot. Cook on low for 6 to 8 hours.

Tracy's Tip...

A leaf of lettuce in a pot of stew absorbs any grease or fat from the top of the pot. After the lettuce leaf is coated, take it out and throw away.

Prep time: 20 minutes • Cook time: 6 to 8 hours • Serves: 6 to 8

Beef and Wild Rice Stew

3 to 4 pounds beef

2 quarts water

2 large white onions, sliced

2 teaspoons salt

1/8 teaspoon pepper, freshly ground

Tracy's Ultimate Seasoning to taste

1 1/2 cups wild rice, washed

Cut beef in 1" cubes and simmer with water and onions in large skillet, uncovered, for about 3 hours.

Mix salt, pepper and Tracy's Ultimate Seasoning to taste. Add, along with wild rice, to beef. Stir mixture and simmer, uncovered, for about 20 minutes more or until rice is tender and most of the liquid is absorbed.

Prep time: 20 minutes • Cook Time: 4 hours • Serves: 8 to 10

Uncle Bill's
Bar-B-Cue Sauce

1/4 cup vinegar

2 teaspoons mustard

1/8 teaspoon Tracy's Garlic Pepper Seasoning Mix

1/2 teaspoon cayenne pepper

1 onion, chopped

1 1/2 teaspoons liquid smoke

1/2 can beer

3/4 teaspoon salt

1/2 cup ketchup

1 thick lemon slice

1/4 cup butter

Combine all ingredients in a saucepan and simmer for 15 minutes, stirring occasionally until thickened.

Prep time: 20 minutes • Cook time: 15 to 20 minutes

Beef Tacos

1 1/2 pounds ground beef

1 Tablespoon vegetable oil

1/2 teaspoon Tracy's Garlic Pepper Seasoning Mix

1 Tablespoon onion, minced

1/2 teaspoon salt

1/2 cup tomato sauce

1 dozen pre-formed taco shells

1 1/2 cups cheddar cheese, grated

1 cup onion, diced

1 cup lettuce, shredded

2 medium tomatoes, diced

3/4 cup taco sauce

Heat oil in skillet. Brown beef in skillet with Tracy's Garlic Pepper Seasoning Mix, onion and salt. Add tomato sauce.

Fill taco shells with beef and top with cheese, onion, lettuce, tomatoes and taco sauce.

Prep time: 10 minutes • Cook Time: 20 minutes • Serves: 4 to 6

Burrito Bake

1 pound ground beef

1 can (16 oz.) refried beans

1 cup biscuit baking mix

1/4 cup water

1 cup thick salsa

1 1/2 cups cheddar cheese, shredded

1 avocado, sliced (optional)

Sour cream (optional)

Preheat the oven to 375°.

In a large skillet, brown the ground beef. In a large bowl, mix the beans, baking mix and water very well. Spread the mixture in the bottom, and half way up the sides, of a greased, 10" pie plate. Add the browned ground beef, salsa, cheese and avocado. Bake for 30 minutes.

Place a dollop of sour cream on each serving, if desired.

Prep time: 5 minutes • Cook time: 40 minutes • Serves: 8

Good Texas Chili

2 pounds ground beef

1 1/4 cups vegetable oil

1 cup onion, chopped

2 garlic cloves, minced

1 large green pepper, cut in strips

3 Tablespoons chili powder

2 teaspoons sugar

3 1/2 cups canned whole tomatoes

1 cup tomato sauce

1 cup water

1/2 teaspoon salt

1 Tablespoon all purpose flour (optional)

2 Tablespoons water (optional)

2 cups kidney beans

Mozzarella or cheddar cheese for topping (optional)

In a large skillet, brown the ground beef in the vegetable oil. Drain off most of the fat. Add the onions, garlic and green pepper to the skillet and sauté 5 minutes, stirring constantly. Add the chili powder, sugar, tomatoes, tomato sauce, water and salt. If a thicker chili is desired, stir in 1 Tablespoon flour mixed with 2 Tablespoons water. Turn heat down and simmer for 30 minutes. Add the beans, stirring to mix them in and let simmer for another 5 to 10 minutes.

Serve topped with grated Mozzarella or cheddar cheese, if desired.

Prep time: 20 minutes • Cook Time: 55 minutes • Serves: 6 to 8

Marinated Dijon Flank Steak

1 1/2 pounds flank steak

1/4 cup lemon juice

2 Tablespoons Worcestershire

2 Tablespoons Tracy's Sweet Southern Dijon Marinade

2 Tablespoons olive oil, divided

1 Tablespoon sugar

3 garlic cloves, chopped

1/2 teaspoon salt

1/4 teaspoon pepper

Combine lemon juice, Worcestershire, Tracy's Sweet Southern Dijon Marinade, 1 Tablespoon olive oil, sugar, garlic, salt and pepper in a shallow dish large enough to hold the steak, stirring to combine. Pierce the steak all over with a fork and toss in marinade. Marinate for 30 minutes, turning once.

In a large skillet, cast iron if you have it, heat 1 Tablespoon of olive oil over high heat until smoking. Remove steak from marinade and cook until browned (about 4 to 5 minutes per side for medium rare). Remove from heat, cover and let stand for 5 minutes.

In a small saucepan, bring the marinade to a boil. Strain into a serving dish, discard the solids and serve over slices of the steak.

Prep time: 30 minutes • Marinate: 30 minutes • Cook time: 10 minutes • Serves: 4

Whiskey Sirloin Roast

1 4-pound sirloin roast

Tracy's Ultimate Seasoning

1/4 cup whiskey

2 Tablespoons Worcestershire

2 cups ketchup

1/4 cup lemon juice

1/2 cup brown sugar

Preheat oven to 350°.

Season roast with Tracy's Ultimate Seasoning and place on a rack in a shallow roasting pan. Combine the remaining ingredients in a saucepan and heat until the brown sugar has melted. Baste the roast with the sauce. Bake at 350° for 2 hours for rare (140° on a meat thermometer) or 2 1/2 hours for medium (160°). Baste frequently with the sauce during cooking.

Prep time: 5 minutes   •   Cook Time: 2 to 2 1/2 hours   •   Serves: 8 to 10

Poultry

NaNa's Last Trip

*U*p until she was 71-years young, my grandma went fishing and hunting. She did it more out of the necessity to eat rather than the sport, although she enjoyed both aspects.

After my career took off I had less time to spend going with her, so I passed the miles away riding on the bus remembering the good times I had over the years with NaNa.

As NaNa got older, and it became harder for her to move around, she had to cut back on the time she spent hunting and fishing. I could hear the disappointment in her voice every time I talked about going and she was unable to join me. So I decided to take her one last time. It was an experience I will never forget.

My good friend Toxey Haas of Mossy Oak Brand Camo® suggested we find a place in south Texas where I could bring NaNa to hunt for wild turkey, something she'd never done before. We'd also tape a show for *Mossy Oak's Hunting the Country* TV series, which made it all the more special to me. NaNa agreed to go and we loaded into my truck and drove eight hours from her home in Vidor, Texas, to the legendary King Ranch.

Any worries I had about NaNa not fitting in were erased when I found her in the kitchen swilling a cold beer and swapping war stories with the ranch hands. After a great cowboy dinner we all headed to bed excited about the opportunities awaiting us at daybreak.

I found NaNa at 4:30 the next morning all decked out in her traditional hunting outfit of a blue flannel shirt and jeans. There wasn't a camouflaged thread in her wardrobe. After much cajoling,

we convinced NaNa to wear some camo and she changed into Mossy Oak's Breakup pattern. Old habits die hard and NaNa wanted to hunt with her trusty shotgun, which was sufficient for hunting critters in her neck of the woods, but not in the turkey country of south Texas. I finally convinced her to leave her beloved gun behind and use one of my new turkey guns.

Wild turkeys are very smart and the wiliest of all game animals, bar none. And they can be easily spooked. When we arrived at our spot, NaNa climbed out of the truck and slammed the door shut, giving the birds a wakeup call. Fortunately, the birds came down from their roosts instead of flying away to the next county. We set up and just as the sun emerged over the rolling hills the turkeys began to gobble. I was able to call three huge gobblers within shooting range and NaNa took her first and only wild turkey. And it was all recorded on videotape.

As we strolled back to the truck later that morning I happened to glance over at NaNa. She wore a look of satisfaction and I thought I saw a tear in her eye, too. I knew she was thinking this might be our last trip together and, although we didn't know it at the time, it did prove to be our last one.

But her legacy lives on in my mind and her love and appreciation of the outdoors will be passed on to my kids.

*

Broiled Wild Turkey

1 turkey, cut up

1 cup butter

1 teaspoon salt

1/2 teaspoon black pepper

Tracy's Mesquite Grill Seasoning

2 cups chicken stock

Preheat broiler.

Rub turkey with butter and sprinkle with salt, pepper and Tracy's Mesquite Seasoning. Place on a well-greased broiler pan and broil for 20 minutes, turning occasionally, until all parts are evenly browned. Remove from oven and turn oven down to 350°.

Place turkey in a baking pan and dot with butter. Add stock, cover tightly and bake at 350° for 30 minutes. Baste several times with liquid in the pan. Serve.

Prep time: 15 minutes • Cook time: 50 minutes • Serves: 4 to 6

South Carolina Duck Bog

2 ducks, whole

6 chicken breasts

14 cups water

1 pound hot sausage

1 pound mild sausage

8 white onions, sliced

5 cups long-grain rice

In a large pot, place the whole skinned ducks and the chicken breasts in the water. Cover and cook over medium heat for about 2 hours, or until the meat separates from the bone easily.

While birds are cooking, brown and crumble sausage in a skillet.

Remove birds, bone completely and return the meat to the pot. Bring to a boil, add onion and the browned and drained sausage and boil for about 5 minutes.

Add 5 cups rice and turn the heat down to low. Cook for about 25 to 30 minutes, checking water level after about 20 minutes, adding more if necessary.

Prep time: 20 minutes   •   Cook Time: 2 to 3 hours   •   Serves: 5

Blackberry Glazed Roasted Cornish Hen

Two Rock Cornish Game Hens

Tracy's Sweet Southern Dijon Marinade

1/2 cup red wine

8 oz. seedless blackberry jam

Place the hens in a large zip-top bag with Tracy's Sweet Southern Dijon Marinade, toss to coat and marinate in refrigerator for about 8 hours.

In a saucepan, cook the wine down for 8 to 10 minutes, add the jam and cook until thick.

Remove the hens, drain and place on the upper level of the grill on very low heat. After a few minutes, baste with the sauce. Turn and baste every 5 minutes or so until done, typically 40 to 60 minutes, depending on the size of the hens.

Prep time: 5 minutes • Marinate: 8 hours • Cook time: 40 to 60 minutes • Serves: 2 to 4

Bourbon Chicken

6 pound mixture of boneless chicken thighs, breast and wings

3/4 cup Tracy's Sweet & Tangy Marinade

1/2 cup bourbon

2 Tablespoons salad oil

2 Tablespoons sugar

1/2 teaspoon ginger

1/3 teaspoon garlic powder

Mix ingredients, pour over chicken and marinate 1 to 2 hours.

Preheat oven to 375°.

Transfer chicken and marinade to a 9x12" baking dish. Bake uncovered 1 1/2 hours at 375°, basting often.

Prep time: 10 minutes • Marinate: 1 to 2 hours • Cook Time: 1 1/2 hours • Serves: 6

Chicken Enchilada Casserole

4 boneless chicken breasts

Salt and pepper

1 medium onion, chopped

3 Tablespoons butter

2 cans cream of chicken soup

1 pint sour cream

1 cup mayonnaise

1 can red chilies

1 can of diced green chilies

8 corn tortillas

16 oz. Mozzarella cheese, grated and divided

Preheat oven to 350°.

Boil chicken in salted and peppered water until done, allow to cool and then coarsely chop. Sauté onions in butter until soft. In large bowl mix soup, sour cream, mayonnaise, red and green chilies and onions. Mix well then add the chicken. Line a 9x13" pan with 4 corn tortillas, spoon 1/2 of the chicken mixture over the tortillas. Sprinkle with 8 oz. of grated cheese. Repeat layers, ending with topping of cheese. Bake 45 minutes at 350°. Top should be slightly browned and bubbly.

Prep time: 10 minutes • Cook time: 1 1/2 hours • Serves: 6 to 8

Broiled Garlic and Herb Chicken

4 boneless chicken breasts

6 Tablespoons salted butter, divided

2 teaspoons lemon juice

1/2 teaspoon salt

1/4 teaspoon white pepper

3 Tablespoons Tracy's Garlic & Herb Marinade

1/4 pound mushrooms, sliced

1/2 cup white wine

Preheat broiler.

Roll the chicken breasts flat. Melt 4 Tablespoons of the butter with the lemon juice, Tracy's Garlic & Herb Marinade, salt and white pepper. Broil the breasts 6 to 8 minutes on each side, basting with the sauce. Sauté the mushrooms in 2 Tablespoons of butter, add the wine and cook down slowly. When the breasts are done, remove to a hot platter and pour the roasting pan drippings into the mushroom blend, stirring to combine. Simmer for 2 to 3 minutes. Pour the combined drippings and mushrooms over the chicken breasts. Serve.

Prep time: 10 minutes • Cook Time: 30 minutes • Serves: 4

Katie's Chicken

1 family pack of boneless, skinless thighs, rinsed and patted dry

1/2 cup cilantro, chopped

2 teaspoons ground ginger

2 bunches green onions, sliced

1 1/2 cups of Tracy's Sweet & Tangy Marinade

1/2 cup rice vinegar

Juice of two limes

6 cloves garlic, crushed

2 teaspoons sesame oil

3 Tablespoons sesame seeds, toasted

1 1/2 teaspoons olive oil

Wash and squeeze cilantro and chop. Combine in a bowl with the ground ginger, green onions, Tracy's Sweet & Tangy Marinade and rice vinegar. Stir to combine. Next add the lime juice, crushed garlic and sesame oil.

Over medium-high heat, brown the sesame seeds in the olive oil. Pour them into the marinade mixture while still hot.

Place chicken thighs into a large dish and pour the marinade over them. They should marinate at least 2 hours, but marinating for closer to 8 hours is best.

Remove chicken thighs and discard marinade. Grill over medium heat until done.

Prep time: 20 minutes • Marinate: 2 to 8 hours • Cook time: 20 to 30 minutes • Serves: 4 to 6

Tarragon Chicken Breasts

4 chicken breasts

1 onion, sliced into thin rings

1 can cream of chicken soup

1/4 teaspoon dried tarragon

1 cup whole milk

1 Tablespoon dried parsley

1 teaspoon Greek seasoning

2 Tablespoons Parmesan cheese

2 cups cooked rice

Preheat oven to 350°.

Remove skin from breasts, place in a baking dish and top with sliced onion rings. Combine the soup, tarragon, milk, parsley and Greek seasoning and mix well. Pour over the chicken, cover and bake for 1 hour at 350°. Remove and sprinkle with the Parmesan cheese. Bake for an additional 10 minutes, uncovered.

Build beds of rice on platters and serve the chicken on top.

Prep time: 20 minutes • Cook Time: 1 1/2 hours • Serves: 4

Orange Chicken

1 whole chicken, cut up

Olive oil

1 onion, finely chopped

1 stalk of celery, finely chopped

1 cup fresh orange juice

1/4 cup grated fresh orange rind

2 Tablespoons Tracy's Ultimate Seasoning

Coat a skillet with olive oil and heat to medium. Slowly brown the chicken parts, turning constantly. Add the onions and celery and continue browning. Pour off any liquid and add orange juice and the grated rind.

Add Tracy's Ultimate Seasoning, cover and simmer over low heat for about an hour, checking occasionally and adding water if necessary.

Tracy's Tip...

This dish tastes great served on a bed of white rice.

Prep time: 10 minutes   •   Cook time: 1 1/2 hours   •   Serves: 4

Chicken Jambalaya

4 chicken breasts

2 teaspoons salt

1/2 teaspoon black pepper

1/2 cup shortening

2 cups chicken broth

1/2 cup white onion, finely chopped

1/4 teaspoon garlic, minced

1/2 cup bell pepper, chopped

1/4 cup water

1 cup uncooked rice

1 bay leaf

1/2 teaspoon chili powder

1/2 teaspoon thyme

1 teaspoon parsley flakes

1/2 cup diced cooked ham

1 cup canned tomatoes

Rub the chicken breasts with salt and pepper. Brown the chicken in shortening in an iron skillet, pour off drippings and add the chicken broth. Cover and simmer slowly over a low heat for about 1 1/2 hours or until the chicken is tender.

Add the onion, garlic and pepper to 1/4 cup of water. Set aside. Add the rice to the amount of water its directions call for; then add the soaking vegetables and cook until the rice begins to stick, stirring constantly.

Remove the chicken and broth from the skillet and combine with the rice mixture in a large pot. Add bay leaf, chili powder, thyme and parsley flakes. Mix lightly, cover and cook on medium-low heat for ten minutes. Add ham and tomatoes, mix again and cook covered for another 10 minutes and serve.

Prep time: 30 minutes • Cook time: 2 hours • Serves: 4 to 6

Grilled Game Hen Dijon

2 dressed Rock Cornish Game Hens

Tracy's Ultimate Seasoning

1/4 onion, finely chopped

1/4 cup pickled jalapeno peppers,
finely chopped

1 clove garlic, minced

2 bacon strips, cut into small pieces

3 Tablespoons Dijon mustard

2 Tablespoons white wine

Tracy's Sweet Southern Dijon Marinade

Skin whole birds and rinse. Sprinkle well with Tracy's Ultimate Seasoning.

Combine onion, peppers, garlic, bacon, Dijon mustard and white wine and blend into stuffing and pack into bird cavity.

Place prepared birds on grill on protective vegetable tray designed for grill to prevent overcooking bottom (back) of birds. Grill on low heat, basting often with Tracy's Sweet Southern Dijon Marinade to keep moist during roasting. Grill time about 40 to 45 minutes.

Serve whole.

Prep time: 20 minutes • Cook Time: 40 to 45 minutes • Serves: 2

Chicken Breasts Dijon

2 skinned and boned chicken breasts (4 halves)

1/2 teaspoon salt

1/4 teaspoon pepper

2 Tablespoons butter

2 Tablespoons virgin olive oil, mixed with basil

1/2 cup onion, chopped

2 garlic cloves, minced

1 cup chicken broth

4 Tablespoons lemon juice

6 Tablespoons Dijon mustard

1 teaspoon dried marjoram

Cooked wild rice

Rub chicken breasts with salt and pepper. Melt butter in a large skillet, add oil and chicken breasts and cook over medium-low heat around 10 minutes or until browned. Combine onion and next 5 ingredients and add to chicken breasts. Bring to a boil and then reduce heat. Simmer 15 to 20 minutes. Serve over the wild rice.

Prep time: 10 minutes   •   Cook time: 30 to 35 minutes   •   Serves: 4

Onion Smothered Chicken

1 chicken, cut up

1 cup flour

Salt

Tracy's Lemon Pepper Seasoning

1/2 cup shortening

2 cups onion, sliced

1 cup milk

Preheat oven to 325°.

Season the flour with salt and Tracy's Lemon Pepper Seasoning and roll the chicken pieces in it until coated well. In a Dutch oven, brown the bird slowly on both sides in hot shortening, turning once. Top with the sliced onions. Pour in the milk and cover tightly. Bake at 325° for about 1 hour.

Prep time: 15 minutes   •   Cook Time: 1 hour 15 minutes   •   Serves: 4 to 5

Stuffed Cornish Hens

4 dressed Rock Cornish Game Hens

Butter

Tracy's Garlic Pepper Seasoning Mix

Paprika

1 package stuffing

2 cups water

2 cups poultry stock

4 Tablespoons soy sauce

1/4 teaspoon sesame oil

6 beef bullion cubes

Preheat oven to 300°

Rub butter on birds and sprinkle each with Tracy's Garlic Pepper Seasoning Mix and paprika. Cook stuffing and fill each bird cavity and place in a roasting pan. Mix water, poultry stock, soy sauce, sesame oil and bullion cubes and add to pan. Cover and bake for 2 hours at 300°. Remove and baste with pan juices and cook for another 30 minutes.

Place on plates and spoon remaining sauce over each bird.

Prep time: 20 minutes • Cook time: 3 hours • Serves: 4

Turkey Breast and Cream Gravy

1 large turkey breast

3 cups milk

1 cup flour

1/2 teaspoon salt

1/2 teaspoon pepper

1 cup vegetable oil

1 teaspoon onion, minced

Cut turkey breast into cubes. Marinate in milk for 4 hours in the refrigerator.   Remove, saving the milk, and roll in flour seasoned with salt & pepper. Brown in oil. Pour off excess oil and add milk from marinade and the minced onion. Simmer until gravy is thick and creamy. Additional flour may be used to thicken gravy.

Prep time: 20 minutes • Marinate: 4 hours • Cook Time: 1 hour • Serves: 4

Island Duck

4 ducks, breasted

8 slices bacon

2 large onions, sliced

1 cup flour

1 Tablespoon Tracy's Ultimate Seasoning

1/2 cup red wine

1/2 cup orange marmalade

Cook bacon in a large skillet until crisp. Remove and reserve. Sauté sliced onions in the bacon fat until soft. Remove and reserve. Dredge duck breasts in flour and Tracy's Ultimate Seasoning. Sauté them in the bacon fat until lightly brown on both sides. Crumble the bacon and return bacon and onion to pan, covering the duck breasts. Combine wine and marmalade in a small bowl, stirring until blended. Pour mixture over all. Cover and simmer on medium heat for 15 to 20 minutes. Duck breasts should be slightly pink in the middle. Place on a warm platter, pour sauce over top and serve.

Prep time: 15 minutes • Cook time: 40 minutes • Serves: 4

Sherried Chicken Breasts

4 chicken breasts, bone in

Salt and pepper to taste

1/2 cup flour

1 stick butter, divided

1 cup green onions, chopped

1/2 cup bell pepper, chopped

4 medium ripe tomatoes, chopped

1 chili pepper, chopped

1 garlic clove, minced

3 cups chicken broth

1 cup cooking sherry

Season chicken breasts with salt and pepper. Roll in flour and fry in 3/4 stick of butter for 20 minutes or until well browned. In another skillet, sauté the chopped vegetables and garlic for about 10 minutes in remaining 1/4 stick of butter. Add the chicken broth and chicken breasts and simmer for 1 hour. Add the sherry and simmer for another 20 minutes.

Prep time: 20 minutes • Cook Time: 2 hours • Serves: 4

Fried Chicken Breasts

4 chicken breasts, split

Tracy's Ultimate Seasoning

3/4 cup plain flour

1/2 cup cornstarch

1/2 teaspoon baking powder

1/2 teaspoon baking soda

1 egg

3/4 cup water

Vegetable oil

Skin and debone breasts, cut into approximately 1/2" strips. Lightly coat with Tracy's Ultimate Seasoning. Mix remaining ingredients well into a batter. Dip the strips into batter, coating well. Fry in hot oil until brown.

Prep time: 20 minutes • Cook time: 1 hour • Serves: 4

Crocked Chicken

2 chickens, deboned and cubed

2 Tablespoons butter

2 carrots, chopped

2 stalks celery, chopped

1/4 cup Burgundy wine

1/4 cup lemon juice

1 Tablespoon Worcestershire

1 clove garlic, minced

1 teaspoon marjoram

1/2 teaspoon pepper

1 teaspoon seasoned salt

4 or 5 drops of Tabasco®

Cooked rice

Brown the chicken cubes in butter. Place carrots and celery in the bottom of a crock pot and place chicken on top. Combine remaining ingredients except rice and pour half of the mixture over the chicken. Cover and cook on low for 8 hours. Add the remaining sauce and cook on high for 30 minutes. Serve with rice.

Prep time: 15 minutes • Cook Time: 8 1/2 hours • Serves: 4

Grilled Game Hen

2 whole, dressed Rock Cornish Game Hens

5 Jalapeno pepper slices

5 bacon slices

For the marinade:

3/4 cup oil

3/4 cup honey

1/2 cup Tracy's Sweet & Tangy Marinade

1/3 cup lemon juice

1/3 teaspoon black pepper

Clean the birds well, rinse and pat dry. Wrap jalapeno slices in bacon and place in the body cavity of each bird. Place birds in a glass dish. Combine all ingredients for the marinade and pour over the over birds and marinate in refrigerator for at least 8 hours.

Place heavy aluminum foil on grate and grill the birds slowly, over low heat, turning and basting often until done.

Tracy's Tip...

On charcoal, hens cook for nearly an hour, but a gas grill might cook a little faster.

Prep time: 20 minutes • Marinate: 8 hours • Cook time: 40 minutes to 1 hour • Serves: 2

Delta Chicken Soup

4 chicken breasts

1 can cream of celery soup

2 cans cream of mushroom soup

2 teaspoons black pepper

1/2 teaspoon salt

1 1/2 cups whole milk

Dash or 2 Tabasco®

Quarter the breasts and parboil for ten minutes. Blend all other ingredients in the pot and simmer for about 30 minutes, stirring occasionally until fully blended.

Serve in bowls.

Prep time: 10 minutes • Cook Time: 45 minutes • Serves: 4

Beaumont's Best Quail

4 quail, skinned and halved

1/4 cup butter

1 can (15 oz.) chopped tomatoes

1 onion, chopped

1/2 teaspoon black pepper

1/2 teaspoon chili powder

1/2 cup green chilies

1/2 teaspoon salt

1/2 teaspoon Tracy's Ultimate Seasoning

1/2 teaspoon cumin

4 slices bacon

2 cups cooked rice

Preheat oven to 350°.

Brown the quail in an iron skillet in the butter and set aside. Mix remaining ingredients together, except bacon and rice. Pour into 2 quart baking dish. Place quail halves in dish and lay bacon slices on top. Cover and bake at 350° for one hour.

Serve with cooked rice.

Prep time: 20 minutes • Cook Time: 1 1/2 hours • Serves: 4

Grilled Chicken Breasts

8 chicken breast halves

1 bottle (16 oz.) Italian dressing

1 Tablespoon Tracy's Ultimate Seasoning

8 thick bacon strips

Wooden toothpicks

Marinate the chicken breasts in the Italian dressing in a glass container in the refrigerator for 6 hours. Remove and sprinkle with Tracy's Ultimate Seasoning. Wrap a bacon strip around each breast and secure with a toothpick.

Grill the breasts over medium heat in a closed grill for about 20 minutes.

Tracy's Tip...

For a different flavor, grill the chicken with smoked hickory chips, or smoke it in a charcoal and water smoker for about 20 minutes.

Prep time: 15 minutes • Marinate: 6 hours • Cook Time: 20 minutes • Serves: 6 to 8

Chicken and Mushrooms

6 chicken breasts

6 slices bacon

Salt and pepper

3 Tablespoons melted butter

1 1/4 pounds mushroom caps, sliced

1 bunch green onions, chopped

2 Tablespoons prepared mustard

1 1/4 teaspoons dry ginger

1 cup orange marmalade

Preheat the oven to 325°.

Wrap the bacon around the chicken breasts and arrange in rows on a large sheet of heavy-duty aluminum foil. Season with salt and pepper to taste. Sauté the mushrooms and green onions in the butter, and pour over the chicken. Seal with a double wrap of foil, and bake for 1 hour at 325°. Combine the mustard, ginger and marmalade and pour over chicken to serve.

Prep time: 20 minutes • Cook time: 1 hour 20 minutes • Serves: 6

Turkey Day at The Beach

$\mathcal{W}$hen I was growing up in southeast Texas our Thanksgiving tradition was to spend the day at my grandma NaNa's house. Everyone gathered around NaNa's buffet-sized dinner table and we'd give thanks for all our many blessings. Then we'd pass around heaping bowls of our Thanksgiving favorites, things like turkey and dressing and a smorgasbord of vegetables picked and canned the previous summer from her bountiful backyard garden. Afterwards, everyone was so full that they'd find a quiet place, take a nap and awake to heat up a plate of leftovers. And then the cycle would repeat itself until it was time to go home. Those are great memories.

Today we do things a little differently. Our family has a beach house on the Gulf of Mexico not far from our home in Beaumont. The atmosphere is not the same as NaNa's house, but it's a great place to unwind and relax on Thanksgiving, especially after I come off a long road trip. The surf is usually calm, the beaches aren't crowded, and the sunsets are incredible. In essence, life slows to a crawl.

My part of the country is known for its gastronomical fusion of Cajun, French and traditional Texas cowboy and Tex-Mex cooking. And some of that culture lands on our dinner table at Thanksgiving. One of my favorite things to prepare is Cajun Fried Turkey. I'm a passionate turkey hunter so I use the wild version when I get lucky, but the store-bought bird will work just as well.

While I'm outside frying the turkey my wife, Michelle, is busy in the kitchen cooking my absolute all time favorite: her Cajun aunt's cornbread dressing. Michelle also fixes up a bunch of our other favorites—sweet potato casserole, fresh fruit salad and cranberry sauce.

Thanksgiving dinner is an all-day affair at the beach. The kitchen opens up early and remains open as long as anybody wants a taste or a second, third or fourth helping of the huge spread of food we so enjoy preparing.

The beach might seem an unlikely place to spend one of our most traditional holidays, but it keeps us grounded in what really matters most. And that is sharing peaceful, memorable moments with family and friends.

*

Cajun Fried Turkey

1 whole turkey, dressed

Tracy's Smokin' Cajun Seasoning

Peanut oil

Heat large fryer with peanut oil to 350°.

Dress the turkey whole, leave skin on. Rub with Tracy's Smokin' Cajun Seasoning.

Slowly lower turkey and cook for 3 minutes per pound plus 5 minutes. Remove, drain, cool and eat.

Prep time: 10 minutes • Cook time: 30 to 40 minutes • Serves: 4 to 6

Evee and her dad season catfish for the stove.

Tracy's cooking gets some close supervision.

Tracy's Blackened Catfish is ready for the table. (recipe, page 140)

The secret ingredient for the "To-Die-For Ribs" is Tracy's seasonings (recipe, page 110).

Tracy gives a slab of ribs a good coating of his Mesquite Grill Seasoning.

The next step to get the ribs ready for the grill is to marinate them with Tracy's Flame Roasted Pepper Marinade, then bake them slowly for a couple of hours.

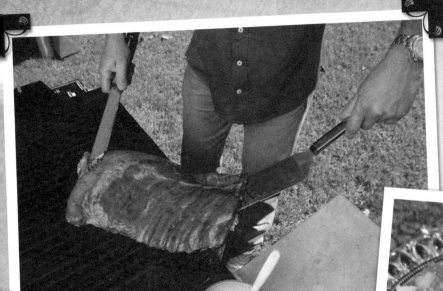

Once out of the oven, the ribs go on the grill over medium heat.

To help seal in taste and moisture, baste the ribs frequently while they cook.

The ribs are ready and they really are "to die for". Creole Potatoes (recipe, page 167) make a great side dish with them, too.

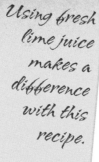

Using fresh lime juice makes a difference with this recipe.

One of Tracy's favorite dishes is his Tequila Lime Shrimp (recipe, page 136).

Tossing all the ingredients by hand makes sure they get well coated.

A good cook always gives the dish a taste test.

102

Great as an appetizer or in tacos, you'll want 10 rounds of Tracy's Tequila Lime Shrimp.

Mustard Fried Tilapia (recipe, page 159) tastes great with a serving of baked beans (recipe, page 178).

Steak Jalapeno (recipe, page 51) is a tasty dish for a backyard cookout.

The game hens need to be grilled over low heat so they don't cook too fast.

Tracy makes sure the Game Hens are well coated with marinade before putting them on the grill.

A Grilled Game Hen Dijon (recipe, page 82) ready for dinner.

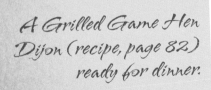

Tracy's Broiled Garlic and Herb Chicken (recipe, page 77) is an easy weeknight dish.

Sweet Taters and Pork Chops (recipe, page 121) is home cooking at its best.

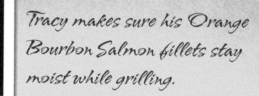

Tracy makes sure his Orange Bourbon Salmon fillets stay moist while grilling.

Salmon on the grill is a quick and easy alternative to burgers or steaks.

A serving of Orange Bourbon Salmon (recipe, page 154) will please most any fish lover.

Pork

BBQ Wars

*I*f you want to start a heated debate in certain regions of the country, namely from North Carolina to Texas, get some local foodies talking about barbecue.

In Texas, barbecued beef brisket is king. There is nothing like pulling up to a Lone Star State institution like the City Market in Luling and eating thinly sliced brisket washed down with a Dr. Pepper (another Texas original). In Texas, to order pork is to commit blasphemy and grounds for being asked to leave the state. You just will not find pig anywhere on the menu. Elsewhere, the opposite holds true.

At the risk of losing my status as a full-blooded, cowboy boot and Stetson hat wearing Texan, I will admit to having eaten the other barbecue. And I have to say, it's not bad.

But unlike us Texans, who know there is only one way to prepare barbecue beef (smoked, over oak, pecan or mesquite wood), the rest of you good people who like the other stuff can't seem to come to terms with how to fix your 'cue. But that's not a bad thing at all, actually. If variety is the spice of life, then pork delivers when it comes to barbecue.

The guys in my band love barbecue and when we can't get the real thing in Texas we search out the best pig joints we can find as we travel the back roads of the South.

We use a grading system to decide whether to stop or keep searching. If the place has smoke slowly rising from a pit then it's a given: we stop. If the joint appears older than dirt then we'll be sure to go in. Signs that show happy dancing pigs or "oink" spelled out in neon in the window are another good catch. What state we're in determines how our pig will get served to us.

If we make our stop in eastern North Carolina it'll be smoked pork mixed with a spicy vinegar sauce without any sign of tomato. One of my favorites …

In central South Carolina the sauce switches to a mustard-based version that adds a tangy and tart flavor to the pork.

When in Memphis the band knows to order a "pig sandwich." That'll be pulled pork on a bun topped with a dollop of coleslaw. But, if you're more in the mood for ribs you can get them served up "wet" or "dry" at places like Corky's and Rendezvous, an old Elvis haunt.

Down in Georgia, stew and pork get married in Brunswick Stew, of which there are as many varieties as Cajun seafood gumbo.

And there you have it. Unlike beef, you can't ruin barbecued pork. The meat will soak up rubs and marinades much better than the real stuff. Did I say that? The debate rages on ...

*"To-Die-For" Bar-B-Q Ribs

Two slabs of pork ribs (about 10 pounds)

Salt and pepper

Tracy's Mesquite Grill Seasoning

Tracy's Flame Roasted Pepper Marinade

Preheat oven to 250°.

Skin the inner membrane from the ribs. Rub ribs with salt, pepper and Tracy's Mesquite Grill Seasoning. Put ribs in disposable baking pans and cover with Tracy's Flame Roasted Pepper Marinade. Seal tightly with foil and bake for 2 hours at 250°.

Remove from pans, put ribs on grill over medium heat, basting occasionally with more marinade. Cook for about one hour with grill lid closed.

Divide ribs and serve.

See how I make these ribs, step-by-step on page 100.

Prep time: 1 hour • Cook time: 3 hours • Serves 6 to 8

Pork Stuffed Cabbage Rolls

1 medium cabbage head

1 pound pork sausage

1/4 pound ground ham

1 cup cooked white rice

1 egg, well beaten

1 onion, finely chopped

1/2 cup milk

1 Tablespoon Tracy's Ultimate Seasoning

1/2 cup water

1 can (8 oz.) tomato sauce

Clean cabbage and remove core. Steam cabbage until the leaves are soft and pliable. Remove and separate the leaves. Set aside the largest 8 for the rolls and keep the others.

Combine the sausage, ham, rice, egg, onion, milk and Tracy's Ultimate Seasoning and mix thoroughly. Using the leaves set aside, fill each with the mixture and roll, tuck in the ends and secure with toothpicks.

Place the stuffed, rolled leaves in a heavy sauce pan, add the water and tomato sauce. Cover with remaining leaves. Cover the saucepan tightly and cook over low heat for about 1 1/2 to 2 hours. Check after an hour and add more water if necessary.

Remove rolls and serve.

Prep time: 15 minutes • Cook time: 2 hours • Serves: 6 to 8

Beer Pork Roast

1 5-pound Boston Butt, deboned

1 large onion, sliced

1/2 cup ketchup

2 Tablespoons brown sugar

1 clove garlic

1 can beer

Salt & pepper to taste

Preheat oven to 250°.

Double heavy duty aluminum foil with enough to wrap the ham. Place the ham in the foil package and top with the onion. Mix ketchup, brown sugar, garlic and beer. Salt and pepper to taste and pour the sauce over the ham. Wrap the foil over and around the ham securely and seal.

Bake for 6 hours at 250°. Remove and slice the ham across the grain and serve with remaining sauce.

Prep time: 20 minutes • Cook Time: 6 hours • Serves: 6 to 8

Boar Burgers

3 pounds ground beef

1 medium onion, chopped fine

1 Tablespoon salt

1 Tablespoon Worcestershire

1 pound ground pork sausage

1 teaspoon black pepper, freshly ground

2 Tablespoons jalapeno hot sauce

1/2 teaspoon garlic powder

Mix all the ingredients very well, shape into big patties and grill. (It's that easy and that good!)

Tracy's Tip...

These burgers taste great with some of my baked beans (recipe on page 178).

Prep time: 15 minutes • Cook time: 20 minutes • Serves: 8

Pork Teriyaki

1 pound ham

For the marinade:

1/4 cup Tracy's Sweet & Tangy Marinade

2 Tablespoons molasses

2 teaspoons ground ginger

1/4 cup oil

2 cloves garlic, minced

2 teaspoons dry mustard

Slice the ham into 6" strips and pound each with a meat tenderizer. Place into a glass dish.

Combine all the ingredients in the marinade and mix well. Then, pour it over the ham and chill in the refrigerator for about 2 to 3 hours. Turn occasionally while it marinades to make sure it gets well coated.

Remove the strips and grill over low heat. This tends to cook fairly fast, so watch the meat and remove earlier than you normally would, about 15 minutes.

Prep time: 20 minutes • Marinate: 2 to 3 hours • Cook Time: 10 to 15 minutes • Serves: 2

Pork Loin Roast

⌒

2 pounds boneless pork loin roast

Tracy's Ultimate Seasoning

Pepper Jelly

Preheat oven to 500° and let it cycle at least twice.

Rinse and pat dry pork loin. Sprinkle generously with Tracy's Ultimate Seasoning to coat all sides and ends. Place loin on a baking rack and transfer to oven. Cook at 500° for 8 minutes.

Leaving roast in closed oven, turn oven off so the total cooking time is 55 minutes. Do not open door until total time is up. Slice in medallions and serve with pepper jelly.

Prep time: 5 minutes • Cook time: 1 hour • Serves: 6 to 8

Pork Sausage Stroganoff

1 pound pork sausage

2 packages Stroganoff mix

1 can green chilies

1 teaspoon crushed cayenne pepper flakes (optional)

1 loaf French bread

Brown and crumble sausage in large skillet. Meanwhile, in a saucepan, prepare the Stroganoff noodles and sauce as directed on the packaging.

Drain sausage and add chilies. Cook a little longer. After the Stroganoff sets, add it to the skillet of sausage, add pepper flakes, blend and serve with French bread.

Prep time: 5 minutes • Cook Time: 20 minutes • Serves: 4 to 6

PORK

Sausage Waffles

1/2 pound pork sausage

1/2 cup water

2 cups flour

1 Tablespoon baking soda

1/2 Tablespoon salt

1 Tablespoon sugar

2 eggs

2 cups milk

1/2 cup melted butter

Brown the sausage in a skillet with the water. Drain and blot dry with paper towels and set aside. In a mixing bowl, combine flour, soda, salt and sugar. Add eggs, milk and butter and blend. Now add the sausage and mix thoroughly. Bake in a waffle iron until golden brown (just as steam stops coming out from the edges you'll know they're done).

Serve with butter and hot syrup.

Prep time: 10 minutes • Cook time: 6 to 8 minutes per waffle • Serves: 2 to 4

Simple Sausage and Bean Stew

16 oz. smoked pork sausage, halved lengthwise and sliced thin

1 can (15 oz.) black beans

1 can (15 oz.) great northern beans

1 can (15 oz.) red kidney beans

1 can (14 1/2 oz.) diced tomatoes

1 can (14 1/2 oz.) chicken broth

2 cloves garlic, minced

1 small onion, diced

1/2 teaspoon oregano

1/2 teaspoon cumin

1/2 teaspoon salt

1/2 teaspoon Tracy's Garlic Pepper Seasoning

Dash or two of Tabasco®

Bring all ingredients to a boil, cover and simmer for 15 minutes and serve. (See, I told you it was simple.)

Prep time: 5 minutes • Cook Time: 30 minutes • Serves: 8 to 10

Breakfast Sausage Casserole

1 pound hot sausage

Vegetable spray

1 large can of Pillsbury® Grands biscuits

1/2 cup cheddar cheese, shredded

5 eggs

Salt and pepper

Tabasco®

Preheat oven to 375°.

Brown the sausage in a skillet. Coat a bundt pan with vegetable spray and press half the can of biscuits flat in the bottom. Sprinkle the cheese over the biscuits, drain the sausage and cover the cheese evenly with sausage. Whip the eggs and pour over the sausage. Salt and pepper to taste and add a few dashes of Tabasco®. Cover with the remaining biscuits. Cook at 375° for 25 to 30 minutes.

Prep time: 10 minutes • Cook time: 45 minutes • Serves: 4 to 5

Ham and Eggs Jambalaya

1/2 stick butter

1 slice ham, diced

1/2 onion, chopped

2 cups cooked white rice

4 eggs

Tabasco®

Salt & pepper

   Melt the butter in an iron skillet and cook the ham and onion in the butter until the onion is soft. Add the cooked rice and stir until hot. Add the eggs and mix well. Add a few dashes of Tabasco® and cook, stirring constantly. When the eggs have blended and cooked, salt and pepper to taste and serve.

Prep time: 10 minutes • Cook Time: 30 minutes • Serves: 4

Sweet 'Taters and Pork Chops

4 thick cut pork chops

2 red pepper pods

1 cup water

1 teaspoon salt

1/4 teaspoon black pepper

1/8 teaspoon sage

2 Tablespoons lemon juice

4 large yams, peeled and quartered

1/4 cup brown sugar

1/2 teaspoon cinnamon

1/8 teaspoon ginger

Place dressed pork chops in a pot with the pepper pods. Cover with cold water and bring to a boil. Simmer for 30 minutes. Remove and place on a rack in a Dutch oven or roasting pan. Add water. Sprinkle with salt, pepper, sage and lemon juice. Place yams around the chops. Combine sugar, cinnamon and ginger and sprinkle on top of yams. Cover and cook over very low temperature on top of stove (or bake at 325°) for 1 hour or until the meat is brown. Serve on a hot platter.

Prep time: 15 minutes • Cook time: 1 1/2 hours • Serves: 4

Pork Chop Potato Bake

6 pork chops

Vegetable oil

Tracy's Ultimate Seasoning

1 can condensed cream of celery soup

1/2 cup whole milk

1/2 cup sour cream

1/2 teaspoon Tracy's Garlic Pepper Seasoning

1 package (24 oz.) frozen hash browns, thawed

1 cup cheddar cheese, grated and divided

1 can French fried onions, divided

Preheat oven to 350°.

Brown pork chops in lightly oiled skillet. Sprinkle with Tracy's Ultimate Seasoning and set aside.

In a bowl, combine soup, milk, sour cream, Tracy's Garlic Pepper Seasoning and 1/2 Tablespoon Tracy's Ultimate Seasoning. Stir in hash browns, 1/2 cup of cheese and 1/2 cup of French fried onions. Spoon mixture into 13x9" glass baking dish and arrange chops over potato mixture.

Bake, uncovered at 350° for 40 minutes. Top with remaining cheese and onions and bake for an additional 5 minutes.

Prep time: 20 minutes • Cook Time: 1 hour • Serves: 6

Marinated Rotisserie Pork Loin

4- to 5-pound pork loin

Tracy's Sweet Southern Dijon Marinade

Tracy's Ultimate Seasoning

Beer

Inject pork loin with Tracy's Sweet Southern Dijon Marinade and rub it well with Tracy's Ultimate Seasoning. Cover and refrigerate overnight. Remove and let sit at least 45 minutes at room temperature before cooking.

Secure loin well centered on grill rotisserie. Place disposable aluminum pan under meat and fill 1/4 full with beer.

Cook over medium low heat, basting every 20 minutes or so with beer, being sure to maintain liquid in drip pan. Loin should cook until inside temperature is 155° to 160 °, approximately 3 to 4 hours.

Let stand 15 minutes before slicing.

Prep time: 20 minutes • Marinate: overnight • Cook time: 3 to 4 hours • Serves: 6 to 8

Stove Top Sausage Casserole

1/2 pound sausage

2 cups frozen shredded hash browns, thawed

1 can tomatoes with diced green chilies

Tracy's Potato Seasoning

8 oz. Velveeta®, diced

6 eggs, beaten

2 Tablespoons milk

In a large skillet, slightly cook the sausage over medium heat. Add hash browns, tomatoes and sprinkle with Tracy's Potato Seasoning to taste. Continue cooking until potatoes have browned. Top with diced cheese.

Mix eggs and milk and pour evenly over sausage mixture. Reduce heat to low, cover and cook for 5 minutes. Remove cover and continue to cook for 7 minutes more.

Prep time: 15 minutes • Cook Time: 12 minutes • Serves: 4 to 6

Link Sausage Casserole

1 package (1 pound) sausage links

1 medium onion, diced

1 medium bell pepper, diced

1 can tomato sauce

Salt and pepper

Tabasco®

Tracy's Smokin' Cajun Seasoning

6 eggs, beaten

Preheat oven to 400°.

Split links length wise and brown on both sides. Remove from skillet and place in a 10x10" greased baking dish. Sauté the onion and bell pepper in sausage drippings until soft. Stir in tomato sauce and season with salt, pepper, Tabasco® and Tracy's Smokin' Cajun Seasoning to taste.

Scramble eggs until almost done. Spoon eggs over sausage and top with sauce mixture.

Bake at 400° for 15 minutes.

Prep time: 15 minutes • Cook time: 45 minutes to 1 hour • Serves: 4 to 6

Easy Roasted Pork Loin

5 to 8 pound pork loin

Tracy's Mesquite Grill Seasoning

1 cup water

Preheat oven to 325°.

Wash pork loin.

Rub liberally with Tracy's Mesquite Grill Seasoning. Place in a greased roasting pan with lid. Add water, cover and cook for 3 to 4 hours.

Let cool 15 minutes before slicing.

Prep time: 5 minutes • Cook Time: 3 to 4 hours • Serves: 6 to 8

Sausage Wrapped Pepper Poppers

12 Anaheim Peppers

8 oz. cream cheese

6 oz. sharp cheddar cheese, grated

1 pound pork sausage

3 to 4 cups Cheeze-its® crackers, finely crushed

Preheat oven to 450°.

Wearing gloves, wash peppers, slice tops off and split lengthwise. Scrape out seeds and veins (a melon baller is great for this). Fill hollowed peppers with cheeses.

Flatten sausage on wax paper with a rolling pin. Cut away enough sausage to cover peppers completely. Wrap the peppers in the sausage then roll them in the crushed Cheeze-its® crackers.

Place in an ungreased glass dish and cook 20 to 30 minutes at 450°. Check after 15 minutes to make sure they aren't browning too fast.

Tracy's Tip...

The first three steps can be done the night before and then just roll the sausage covered peppers in the crumbs right before cooking.

Prep time: 40 minutes • Cook time: 20 to 30 minutes • Serves: 6

Stove Top Pork Chops

6 1" thick pork chops

1/2 cup brown sugar

1/2 teaspoon salt

1/2 teaspoon pepper

1 teaspoon Tracy's Mesquite Grill Seasoning

All purpose flour

Oil

1 yellow onion, peeled and sliced

Water

Combine sugar, salt, pepper and Tracy's Mesquite Grill Seasoning; rub into pork chops and then coat them with flour.

Heat enough oil in a deep skillet to brown the chops. After browning, cover pork chops with onion slices. Add water to cover chops and onions, reduce heat to simmer and cook for about 1 1/2 hours or until they almost fall apart. (You may need to add a little bit more water about halfway through.)

Prep time: 15 minutes • Cook Time: 1 1/2 hours • Serves: 6

Fruit Stuffed Pork Chops

6 1" thick boneless pork chops

1 cup chopped pineapple

1 teaspoon curry powder

Cut a pocket into each pork chop. Mix the chopped pineapple and curry; stuff each pork chop with fruit mixture and grill away from flame for approximately 1 hour, turning once.

Tracy's Tip...

Orange Candied Yams (recipe, page 176) makes a great side dish for these pork chops.

Prep time: 25 minutes • Cook time: 1 hour • Serves: 6

Marinated Pork Roast

3 pounds pork loin roast

8 oz. Tracy's Rotisserie Garlic & Herb Marinade

2 Tablespoons oregano

1/2 teaspoon salt

1/2 teaspoon pepper

Preheat oven to 375°.

Wash roast and pierce with small paring knife. Place in large zip-top plastic bag and pour marinade over roast. Marinate overnight in refrigerator, turning occasionally.

Before cooking, drain roast and discard marinade. Pat dry and rub in oregano, salt and pepper. Bake 1 hour at 375° or until meat thermometer reads 155°.

Let stand 15 minutes before slicing.

Prep time: 20 minutes   •   Marinate: overnight   •   Cook Time: 1 hour   •   Serves: 4 to 6

Creole Sausage and Potatoes

2 Idaho potatoes, cubed to about 1"

1 1/2 pounds smoked sausage, cut to bite size

1 cup fresh mushrooms, small

1 large white onion, chopped coarse

1 red and/or green bell pepper, sliced

2 celery sticks, cut to 1" pieces

Tabasco®

1/4 stick butter

Salt & pepper

Several dashes Worcestershire

Line a large bowl with heavy aluminum foil, using two or more sheets and leaving extra foil outside bowl. Then mix all ingredients in bowl, adding salt, pepper and Tobasco® to taste. Wrap loosely in the foil and seal.

Grill on medium low heat for 45 minutes to 1 hour, occasionally turning and shaking to blend butter and spices.

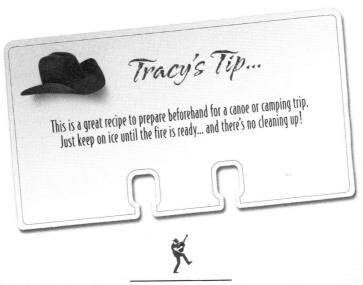

Tracy's Tip...

This is a great recipe to prepare beforehand for a canoe or camping trip.
Just keep on ice until the fire is ready... and there's no cleaning up!

Prep time: 30 minutes • Cook time: 45 minutes to 1 hour • Serves: 4

Red Beans and Rice Roulet

1 pound dried red beans

1 large yellow onion, chopped

1 can tomato sauce

1 1/2 teaspoons garlic powder

1/4 cup parsley, chopped

1 1/2 teaspoons thyme

1 Tablespoon salt

1/4 teaspoon cayenne pepper

1/4 teaspoon Tracy's Smokin' Cajun Seasoning

1 pound smoked sausage, sliced

3 quarts water

Tabasco®

1/2 pound ground beef

1 1/2 teaspoons chili powder

1 bottle beer

steamed white rice

Soak beans overnight.

In a large pot (1 gallon or more) combine all ingredients except ground beef, chili powder, beer and rice. Bring to a boil, then reduce heat and cover. Simmer for 3 hours or until beans are cooked.

Brown the ground beef and add it to the pot along with the chili powder. Cook for another 30 minutes. Add 1 bottle of beer and heat through. When heated, serve over steamed white rice.

_____

Prep time: 20 minutes • Cook Time: 3 1/2 hours • Serves: 5 to 6

Fish

The One that Got Away

My grandma did a little bit of everything to make ends meet. When I was in the sixth grade she had a landscape business and I helped her mow yards during my summer vacation.

One morning I had to get started especially early, but I didn't mind at all. We needed to finish up as quickly as we could so we could head out on a week-long camping and fishing trip to Toledo Bend Reservoir, which, at the time, was my favorite place on the entire planet.

The last stop of the morning was at the Bonus Burger in my hometown of Vidor, Texas. By the time we had gotten the mowers unloaded and were ready to cut the grass, my mind was already halfway to Toledo Bend. As I began mowing I could see NaNa's car out of the corner of my eye. Strapped to the roof was her 12-foot johnboat with the 4 h.p. outboard motor with all our tackle and camping gear packed in the trunk. I was ready to get the grass cut and get out of town.

Needless to say, I should have been paying more attention to what I was doing. As I was mowing the dew-coated hillside my foot slipped and went beneath the lawnmower. NaNa rushed to my side, picked me up, put me in the car and we sped off to the emergency room.

The throbbing pain in my big toe was overridden by the thought of missing our trip to my favorite place on the planet. After the doctor had finished bandaging me up I mustered up the courage to ask the dreaded question: "Can we still go fishing?" Seeing that I was about to cry, the doctor told NaNa yes, but only if I kept the bad foot elevated. I was relieved and thrilled. I climbed into the back seat of NaNa's car and propped my foot up on the front console and we headed east.

We headed off through the Texas piney woods

FISH

and arrived a couple hours later at Toledo Bend, a sprawling impoundment located on the Texas-Louisiana border and renowned for its trophy bass fishing.

Before we left town that afternoon, my dad told me that if I caught a largemouth bass weighing more than six pounds he would have it mounted. Knowing this made me more determined than ever to catch a lunker and not even a bad foot could dampen my spirits.

NaNa slipped the boat into the lake, I hopped aboard and propped my foot up on the ice chest. We weaved through the timber-lined creek and out into the main lake, headed towards my favorite lunker hole.

When we arrived at the spot I began chunking away with a topwater lure and on about the fifth cast I connected with the big one. I could tell the fish easily weighed six pounds by the way it nearly snapped my rod. After it cleared the surface a few times I finally got it to the boat and NaNa netted my trophy for me.

Back at the marina we hauled the catch up to the scales. I couldn't believe it. My big catch weighed in at 5 3/4 pounds—just shy of the six pound mark.

So I didn't get my mount on that trip, but like NaNa said, "It ain't called catching ... it's called fishing."

Tequila Lime Shrimp

2 pounds medium shrimp

1 shot tequila

1 Jicama, finely chopped

1 bunch of cilantro, finely chopped

1 medium yellow onion, finely chopped

1/2 cup vegetable oil

Juice of 1 lime

Boil the shrimp, then cool and peel. Mix the other ingredients into a marinade and pour into a zip-top bag with the cooled and peeled shrimp; chill for two hours.

Serve the shrimp as an hors d'oeuvre or warm them and try them as a taco filling in a corn or flour tortilla. If you use them in a taco, add purple and green cabbage and Pico de Gallo.

Prep time: 30 minutes • Marinate: 2 hours • Cook Time: 15 minutes • Serves: 5 to 6

Biloxi Bay Seafood Gumbo

1/2 cup extra virgin olive oil with basil
1/2 cup all purpose flour
2 cups white onion, chopped
2 garlic cloves, minced
1 cup bell pepper, chopped
1 cup celery, chopped
1 cup okra, sliced
3 cups tomatoes, chopped
1 teaspoon salt
1 teaspoon Tabasco® (red)
1 teaspoon Tabasco® (green)
1 teaspoon Tracy's Smokin' Cajun Seasoning
2 bay leaves
6 cups water
1 bottle (16 oz.) beer
1 pound medium shrimp, peeled
1/2 pound crabmeat
1 pint oysters with liquor or 1 dozen shucked with liquor
8 oz. flounder, cubed
1/4 cup green onions, chopped
1 Tablespoon filè
1/4 cup parsley, chopped
cooked rice

Combine the oil and flour in a large cast iron skillet over medium heat, stirring constantly until mixture turns into a brown roux. In a large pot, combine roux, onions, garlic, bell pepper, celery, okra, tomatoes, salt, Tabasco® (red and green), Tracy's Smokin' Cajun Seasoning and bay leaves.

Stir over medium low heat until very soft (10 to 15 minutes). Add water and beer and blend with roux. Reduce heat and simmer on low, uncovered, for about 1 1/2 hours.

Add shrimp and crabmeat, cook about 20 minutes, still on low. Add oysters and flounder, along with green onions, filè and parsley and cook for 5 more minutes, slightly raising heat.

Remove bay leaves; serve in bowls mixed with rice.

Prep time: 45 minutes • Cook time: 2 hours • Serves: 8

Logan's Cheddar Catfish

Sometimes playing around in the kitchen can invent a good meal, even if it sounds odd. This is one of those dishes.

4 catfish filets

Cheeze-its® Crackers

Whole milk

Preheat oven to 350°.

Crush a half-box of Cheez-its® into fine crumbs. Rinse fillets, dip in milk and coat with Cheeze-its® crumbs. Place fillets on baking sheet in oven for about 10 to 12 minutes at 350° or until flakey. Don't overcook.

Prep time: 10 minutes • Cook Time: 10 to 12 minutes • Serves: 4

FISH

Hushpuppies

1/2 Tablespoon vegetable oil

1 egg

2 large onions, chopped

3 cups self-rising cornmeal

1 cup self-rising flour

1 Tablespoon sugar

1 teaspoon baking powder

1 Tablespoon salt

1 teaspoon ground black pepper

2 teaspoons Tracy's Garlic Pepper Seasoning Mix

1 1/2 cups milk

Preheat oil in a pan to 350° to 375°.

Mix egg and chopped onion in bowl. Add cornmeal, flour, sugar, baking powder and remaining spices. Stir and slowly add milk until blended. With a little oil on a teaspoon and your finger, slide one spoonful of hushpuppy batter at a time into the hot oil, turning once, until golden brown.

Tracy's Tip...

When cooking hushpuppies with fried fish, always cook the fish first, followed by the hushpuppies in the same oil. You can keep the fish warm in the oven at 200° on baking sheets lined with brown paper bags, leaving the door slightly open so they won't get soggy while the hushpuppies cook.

Prep time: 20 to 25 minutes • Cook time: 30 minutes • Serves: 6 to 8

Tracy's Blackened Catfish

1 1/2 pounds catfish fillets

4 Tablespoons unsalted butter

3 Tablespoons oregano

2 Tablespoons Tracy's Ultimate Seasoning

2 Tablespoons Tracy's Garlic Pepper Seasoning Mix

6 Tablespoons Tracy's Smokin' Cajun Seasoning (or 4 if you like it milder)

Mix all the seasonings well. Melt the butter and dip the fillets. Coat well with the seasoning mixture.

Heat iron skillet on high, then cook catfish fillets 3 minutes on each side. Serve with lemon wedges.

Prep time: 10 minutes • Cook Time: 6 minutes • Serves: 4

Stuffed Flounder Albermarle

3 or 4 large flounder (3/4 to 1 pound each)

2 Tablespoons bacon drippings

1 medium onion, chopped

1 shallot, chopped

2 cloves garlic

2 Tablespoons celery, chopped

2 Tablespoons bell pepper, chopped

1 egg

1 teaspoon salt

1/2 teaspoon pepper

Dash Tabasco®

1/8 teaspoon thyme

1 cup crab meat

1 teaspoon parsley, chopped

3/4 cup bread crumbs

1 stick butter

Preheat oven to 375°.

Sauté vegetables and garlic in bacon drippings, whip egg and mix in next 7 ingredients to make stuffing. Slit a large pocket in each fish. Place generous amounts of stuffing into each pocket. Melt butter in pan. Lay fish in pan, white side down, being sure to not overlap them. Brush some of the melted butter on top (dark) side. Cover and bake at 375° for 20 to 30 minutes. Uncover for the last 5 to10 minutes. Garnish with parsley, serve with lemon halves.

Prep time: 30 to 35 minutes • Cook time: 20 to 30 minutes • Serves: 4

Seafood Chowder

2 large onions, chopped

1/8 pound butter

8 oz. cream cheese

1 can (10 3/4 oz.) cream of potato soup

1 can (10 3/4 oz.) cream style corn

1 can water (use the empty corn can to measure)

1 pound crab meat
or :
{
2 cans (6 1/2 oz.) small shrimp
2 cans (6 1/2 oz.) crab meat
2 cans (6 1/2 oz.) small clams
}

3 pints half & half

Salt and cayenne pepper

Sauté onions in butter. Add cream cheese and soften. Add potato soup, corn and water and cook on medium until well blended. Add crab meat, half & half and then salt and cayenne pepper. Reduce heat and simmer (do not boil) for 15 minutes.

Prep time: 20 minutes • **Cook Time: 30 to 40 minutes** • **Serves: 8**

Brandied Brown Trout

4 14 to 16" brown (or rainbow) trout, whole

2 cups all purpose flour

1 Tablespoon thyme

1 Tablespoon rosemary

Salt and pepper

2 Tablespoons extra virgin olive oil

1/4 cup butter

1/4 cup brandy

Combine flour, thyme and rosemary in a brown paper bag. Season trout well inside and out with salt and pepper. Place each trout in the paper bag and shake to coat well with the seasoning mixture, remove and tap off excess. Heat oil and butter together in large skillet over medium-high heat. Add trout and brown on each side until skin is slightly crisp. Add brandy and cover skillet, reduce heat to medium and cook for 5 to 6 minutes. Serve on platters with skillet juices poured over fish. Garnish with thin lemon slices.

Tracy's Tip...

When handling something slippery like trout, wet your hands and sprinkle them with salt. This helps you get a better grip.

Prep time: 20 minutes • Cook time: 20 to 25 minutes • Serves: 4

Margarita Trout Almondine

4 medium rainbow trout, butterflied

1 can frozen Bacardi® Margarita Mix concentrate, divided

1/2 cup butter

Tracy's Smokin' Cajun Seasoning

Lemon pepper

1/4 cup sliced almonds

In a shallow dish or pan, place butterflied trout (meat side down) in 3/4 can of frozen margarita mix and set aside for about 20 to 30 minutes. Heat and blend remaining 1/4 of concentrate with 1/2 cup butter.

Season trout with Tracy's Smokin' Cajun Seasoning and lemon pepper and place on low heat, skin down. Baste with butter and margarita mix after a few minutes. After about 10 minutes, place sliced almonds on trout and baste again with mix. Trout should not be turned, and should be cooked slowly. Remove when done, about 15 to 20 minutes.

Prep time: 20 minutes   •   Cook Time: 20 minutes   •   Serves: 4

FISH

No-Mess Grilled Crappie

12 crappie fillets with skin attached

4 Tablespoons butter

Tracy's Flame Roasted Pepper Marinade

Salt and pepper

Place aluminum foil on top of grill and poke holes through the foil. Heat the butter and lightly brush it on the fish. Place the fillets on the foil, skin side down, and baste with Tracy's Flame Roasted Pepper Marinade. Salt and pepper to taste. Cook fillets until they are flaky and separated from the skin.

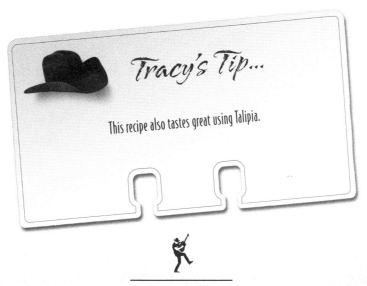

Tracy's Tip...

This recipe also tastes great using Talipia.

Prep time: 5 minutes • Cook time: 10 to 12 minutes • Serves: 4 to 6

Rainbow Trout Provencale

4 rainbow trout fillets (about 4 oz. each)

2 Tablespoons butter

1 bell pepper, julienned

2 cloves garlic, finely chopped

1/2 medium onion, cut into strips

6 Tablespoons dry vermouth or white cooking wine

2 Tablespoons tomato paste

2 Tablespoons fresh parsley, chopped

Salt and pepper

Preheat oven to 300°.

Combine the butter and next three ingredients and sauté well. Stir in vermouth, tomato paste and parsley. Season with salt and pepper.

Place trout fillets meat side down on vegetable mixture in a baking dish. Cover and bake at 300° for about 20 minutes or until flaky.

Place trout on serving plates and top with sauce. Garnish with additional parsley. Serve with lemon wedge.

Prep time: 20 minutes • Cook Time: 20 minutes • Serves: 4

Fantastic Fish Cakes

4 cups fish fillets, cubed

Liquid crab boil

2 eggs

1 cup seasoned Italian bread crumbs

1/2 teaspoon salt

1/4 teaspoon black pepper

1 teaspoon Worcestershire

1 teaspoon dry mustard

1/4 cup mayonnaise

1/4 cup peanut or vegetable oil

Par-broil the fish in liquid crab boil.

Mix the eggs with the breadcrumbs, salt, pepper, Worcestershire, mustard and mayonnaise. Fold in the fish and mold into cakes.

Fry in hot oil in a frying pan for about 5 minutes on each side. They should be browned, but not dried out or soggy.

Tracy's Tip...

These can easily be made ahead of time and heated when ready.

Prep time: 20 minutes • Cook time: 20 minutes • Serves: 4 to 6

Earl's Tomato Fish Stew

2 to 4 pounds fish fillets, cubed

1 pound bacon

2 celery sticks, chopped

3 white onions, diced

1 green bell pepper, chopped

1 red bell pepper, chopped

1 can (10 oz.) of tomato soup

6 oz. ketchup

Salt and pepper

Tabasco®

Tracy's Ultimate Seasoning

1 jar pimentos, diced

Begin frying bacon in large skillet. While it is cooking, add the celery, onion and bell peppers to the frying bacon. Cover and simmer for about 10 minutes. In a large pot, mix the tomato soup with ketchup and heat until thickened. Salt and pepper the fish cubes and add to the soup along with the vegetables and bacon. Add a dash of Tabasco® and Tracy's Ultimate Seasoning to taste. Then add the diced pimentos.

Cover and simmer 1 hour. Serve hot.

Prep time: 25 minutes • Cook Time: 1 1/2 hours • Serves: 8 to 10

Sassy Shrimp

2 pounds large shrimp, peeled and de-veined

4 Tablespoons Tabasco®

1/2 stick unsalted butter, melted

1 teaspoon garlic salt

1/2 cup lemon juice

Combine Tabasco®, butter and garlic salt and mix well. Marinate shrimp in it for 2 hours. Heat until butter melts again and drain, reserving the sauce. Place shrimp on skewers and grill over medium heat for about 3 minutes on each side. Add lemon juice to the sauce and use to baste the shrimp while grilling, brushing evenly over the kebabs.

Prep time: 20 minutes • Marinate: 2 hours • Cook time: 6 minutes • Serves: 4 to 6

Saturday Night Shrimp Dip

2 pounds cooked shrimp, peeled and chopped

1/4 cup lemon juice

3/4 teaspoon horseradish

1/2 cup celery, chopped

1 Tablespoon Worcestershire

1 package (8 oz.) cream cheese

1/2 cup mayonnaise

1 Tablespoon onion, chopped

2 hard boiled eggs, chopped

Salt and pepper

Mix all ingredients well, adding salt and pepper to taste. Chill for 1 hour. Serve dip in bowls.

Prep time: 10 minutes • Cook Time: 10 minutes • Serves: 11

Beer Broiled Shrimp

2 pounds large shrimp, peeled

3/4 cup beer

2 Tablespoons parsley, chopped

1 clove garlic, minced

1/8 teaspoon pepper

3 Tablespoons cooking oil

4 teaspoons Worcestershire

1/2 teaspoon salt

Preheat broiler.

Combine all the ingredients except shrimp in a medium saucepan and mix well. Add the shrimp and stir. Cover and let stand at room temperature for 1 hour. Drain, reserving the sauce. Place shrimp on a well greased boiler rack and broil 6" from heat for 4 minutes. Turn and brush with the sauce. Broil for another 2 minutes or until bright pink.

Prep time: 10 minutes • Cook time: 6 minutes • Serves: 4 to 6

Lemon Pepper Shrimp

2 pounds fresh shrimp, unpeeled

2 Tablespoons Tracy's Lemon Pepper Seasoning

2 sticks butter

Preheat oven to 400°.

Put the shrimp on a baking sheet and sprinkle heavily with Tracy's Lemon Pepper Seasoning. Melt the butter and pour over the seasoned shrimp. Cover with foil and bake at 400° for about 10 minutes. Turn and bake for another 5 minutes. When done, pour the juices over the shrimp, let them cool before serving. Peal and eat.

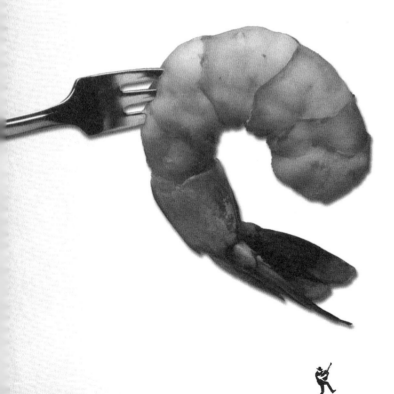

Prep time: 5 minutes • Cook Time: 15 minutes • Serves: 6 to 8

FISH

Shrimp Teriyaki Kabobs with Portobellos

8 oz. medium shrimp, peeled and de-veined

1 package (16 oz.) whole Portobello caps, quartered

1 Tablespoon Tracy's Sweet & Tangy Marinade

1 green bell pepper, quartered

1 red bell pepper, quartered

1 medium onion, cut into chunks about 1/2" thick

1 Tablespoon cornstarch mixed with 1/3 cup cold water

For the marinade:

1/4 cup soy sauce

1/4 cup dry sherry

Juice of 1 lemon

2 Tablespoons sugar

1/4 teaspoon roasted sesame oil

Brush the Portobello pieces with Tracy's Sweet & Tangy Marinade. Then, using 4 skewers, alternate the pieces of mushrooms, peppers and onion with the shrimp. Make a marinade by combining soy sauce, sherry, lemon juice, sugar and sesame oil, stirring well to dissolve the sugar.

Place the prepared skewers in a shallow dish and pour the marinade over them. Let stand for 10 to 20 minutes, basting frequently. Drain and pour marinade into a saucepan. Bring to a boil and thicken with the cornstarch mixture until the sauce coats a spoon. Remove from heat.

Over low heat, grill the skewers until the shrimp are done and the mushrooms have begun to wrinkle, about 3 to 4 minutes on each side. (Or in an oven, preheat to 350°, place the skewers on an oven rack or over a pan and bake for about 6 to 8 minutes.) Remove the shrimp and vegetables from the skewers and put onto serving plates. Pour the sauce over all.

Prep time: 40 minutes • Cook time: 8 to 10 minutes • Serves: 2 to 4

Grilled Orange Bourbon Salmon

4 (6 oz.) salmon fillets, about 1" thick

1/4 cup bourbon

1/4 cup orange juice

1/4 cup low-sodium soy sauce

1/4 cup brown sugar, packed

1/4 cup green onions, chopped

3 Tablespoons fresh chives, chopped

3 Tablespoons lemon juice

2 garlic cloves, chopped

Cooking spray

Combine all ingredients (except the catfish) in a large zip-top bag. Add catfish and marinate in refrigerator 1 1/2 hours, turning bag occasionally. Remove catfish from bag and reserve marinade. Grill catfish on a grill rack or broiler pan coated with cooking spray. Cook 6 minutes on each side or until fish flakes easily when tested with a fork. Baste frequently with reserved marinade.

Prep time: 20 minutes • Marinate: 1 1/2 to 2 hours • Cook Time: 12 to 16 minutes • Serves: 4

Crawfish Etouffee

2 pounds crawfish tails, cooked

3 sticks butter, divided

1 large onion, chopped

2 large bell peppers, chopped

1 stalk celery, chopped

1 bunch green onions, chopped

1 can (10 oz.) cream of mushroom soup

1 cup water

Garlic powder

Salt and pepper

Cayenne pepper

2 cups cooked white rice

Melt 1 stick of butter and sauté the onion, peppers, celery and green onions until tender. Put in a pot and add the cooked crawfish tails. Add the soup, water and the remaining 2 sticks of butter (do not substitute margarine). Cook over low heat until the soup and butter blends to a broth. Then, bring to a brisk boil, stirring continuously for 5 minutes, adding a little more water if necessary.

Remove from heat and add spices to taste, remembering this dish is supposed to have a bite. Serve over white rice.

Prep time: 15 minutes • Cook time: 15 minutes • Serves: 4 to 6

Crawfish Jambalaya

2 pounds crawfish

1/2 cup butter

1 medium onion, chopped

1/2 cup celery with leaves, chopped

1/2 cup green pepper, chopped

1 Tablespoon chili powder

1 teaspoon cumin

1 teaspoon Tracy's Smokin' Cajun Seasoning

1/4 cup flour

1 large can stewed tomatoes

2 Tablespoons Worcestershire

2 cups cooked white rice

Peel crawfish and set aside. In a large skillet, melt the butter and sauté the onion, celery and pepper. When soft, add chili powder, cumin, Tracy's Smokin' Cajun Seasoning and flour. Stir constantly over medium heat until the flour turns a light brown. This makes a roux. Add stewed tomatoes and Worcestershire, stirring to combine. Add crawfish tails and simmer, uncovered, for 20 minutes. Add 2 cups cooked white rice and heat for an additional 3 to 5 minutes.

Prep time: 10 minutes • Cook Time: 35 minutes • Serves: 4 to 6

FISH

Broiled Speckled Trout

4 (6 oz.) speckled trout fillets

1 bottle Italian salad dressing

1/2 stick butter, melted

1 lemon, sliced thin

1/2 cup lemon juice

Paprika and parsley for garnish

Marinate fillets in the salad dressing in a glass container for 2 to 3 hours. Remove fillets and place on a baking sheet with aluminum foil coated with cooking spray. Lightly spread butter on top and cover with lemon slices.

Broil for 8 to 10 minutes or until lightly browned. Remove from oven, garnish with paprika and parsley sprigs. Serve.

Prep time: 5 minutes • Marinate: 2 to 3 hours • Cook time: 8 to 10 minutes • Serves: 4

Oystered Redfish

4 pounds redfish fillets

2 cups white wine

1/2 cup water

4 Tablespoons horseradish sauce

1 Tablespoon butter, melted

4 dashes Tabasco®

2 Tablespoons Worcestershire

1/4 teaspoon black pepper, freshly cracked

1 1/2 teaspoons lemon juice

1 can smoked oysters, chopped (reserve oil)

Preheat oven to 375°.

Place all but about 1/2 pound of the redfish fillets in a baking dish and pour the wine over it. Bake at 375° for 12 to 15 minutes.

Cube and steam the remaining 1/2 pound of the redfish over 1/2 cup boiling water for about 5 minutes. Then, put the steamed cubed redfish, remaining water, horseradish sauce, butter, Tabasco®, Worcestershire, pepper and lemon juice in a blender and puree for about 2 minutes.

Pour the blended mixture into the saucepan over the redfish fillets and return to the oven for 5 minutes. While the fish are cooking, open the oysters, chop well, and then stir them in leftover oil from the can. Remove the redfish from the oven, place on serving plates and top with the oyster sauce.

Prep time: 15 minutes • Cook Time: 30 minutes • Serves: 8 to 10

Mustard Fried Tilapia

4 tilapia fillets

4 Tablespoons Dijon mustard

Stone ground yellow cornmeal

Salt and pepper to taste

Peanut oil

Wash fish and pat dry. Spread both sides lightly with mustard. Roll in cornmeal seasoned with salt and pepper. Place the fish on cake rack to set the cornmeal coating while oil is heating. Heat enough peanut oil in the skillet to cover the fish. When the oil is very hot, fry fish quickly until golden brown, turning once.

Serve with lemon halves.

Prep time: 20 minutes • Cook time: 8 to 10 minutes • Serves: 4

Baked Snook in Cheese Sauce

4 small snook fillets

3 Tablespoons butter

3 Tablespoons flour

1/2 teaspoon dry mustard

Dash of cayenne pepper

1 teaspoon salt

1/4 teaspoon dried dill weed

1 1/2 cups half and half

1 1/2 cups medium cheddar cheese, shredded

4 oz. small salad shrimp

Preheat oven to 400°.

Cut the snook fillets into serving pieces and arrange in a single layer in a greased 2 quart baking dish. In a saucepan, melt the butter and stir in the flour. Cook until bubbly, stirring constantly. Add the next 4 ingredients, remove from heat and stir in half and half. Return pan to the heat, stirring until thick. Mix in 1 cup of cheese and the shrimp. Pour the cheese sauce over the fish, sprinkle with the remaining cheese and bake at 400° for about 15 to 20 minutes.

Prep time: 20 minutes • Cook Time: 20 minutes • Serves: 4

Baked Sardis Crappie

6 to 8 crappie fillets

1 Tablespoon lemon juice

1 teaspoon Worcestershire

1 Tablespoon Parmesan cheese, grated

1/4 cup butter, melted

2 teaspoons onion powder

1 Tablespoon bread crumbs

1/4 teaspoon black powder

Preheat oven to 400°.

Mix all the ingredients (except crappie) well. Place the crappie on a double layer of heavy duty aluminum foil. Pour the mixture over the fish and seal the foil into an air tight pouch. Bake at 400° for 30 minutes. Remove and serve.

Prep time: 10 minutes • Cook time: 30 minutes • Serves: 6

Catfish Gumbo

2 catfish fillets, cubed

1 cup roux

2 cups water

1 onion, chopped

1/4 bell pepper, chopped

1 rib celery, chopped

2 Tablespoons green onion tops, chopped

1 Tablespoon parsley, minced

Salt, pepper and red pepper

Cooked white rice

Put roux in pot with the water and place on medium-high heat; stir. Add onion, pepper, celery, onion tops and parsley. Season with salt, black and red pepper to taste. Bring to a boil, reduce heat to medium and cook for about 1 hour. Add cubed fish and cook only until catfish is tender. Serve in gumbo bowls with cooked rice.

Tracy's Tip...

For added flavor, you can add shrimp, oysters, crawfish and/or crabmeat when adding catfish.

Prep time: 15 to 20 minutes • Cook Time: 1 1/2 hours • Serves: 4

Vegetables

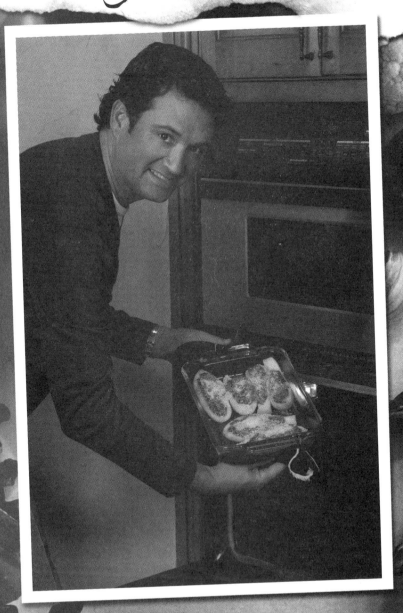

The Tomato Growing Contest

After crossing the invisible dividing line that separates rural America from suburbia you begin to see and feel a change in the landscape. The water and air are cleaner, the people are downright friendlier and life moves at a slower pace.

The landscape of rural America is still grounded in many of life's simple pleasures: the courthouse square where the old timers meet daily to solve the world's problems, and the quaint houses where people wave at passersby while rocking in the front porch swing.

And because the houses aren't stacked on top of each other, there are backyard gardens - some of my favorite places to visit when I can spare the time while on the road. And what a kitchen is to a woman, the backyard garden is to a man. In tiny towns, both places are where social status is measured and personal pride is put on the line with each cake baked and every vegetable picked.

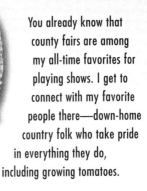

You already know that county fairs are among my all-time favorites for playing shows. I get to connect with my favorite people there—down-home country folk who take pride in everything they do, including growing tomatoes.

Growing tomatoes is an art in tiny towns. Many of the tiny towns I visit hold tomato growing contests at their county fairs. I have even been fortunate enough to have been invited to judge a few of these contests. While the wives are fussing over who will win the baking contest, I'm hanging out with their anxious husbands in the tomato tent where some of the biggest, juiciest tomatoes you will ever see are weighed, sliced and tested by the panel of judges.

The competition begins during the dead of winter when the seed company catalogs are delivered to mailboxes after Christmas. Like a college student cramming for a final exam, the serious growers study the pages with the same intensity, looking for the latest disease resistant hybrid that will give them an edge. There aren't many secrets in small towns, but who is going to grow what is one of the few mysteries that remain.

The serious tomato man suffers through the winter months waiting until the ground is warm enough to turn the garden. Seedlings are grown inside the house safely out of view from the neighbors until, finally, the big day arrives and the plants go into the ground. For the remainder of spring and well into the summer, the plants are meticulously cared for with the same tenderness and affection he has for his grandkids.

By August it's time to determine bragging rights for the year at the county fair. After judging some of these contests I can tell you this is serious business for these people. And the best part of judging the contest is sampling the goods.

Have you ever had a really good tomato sandwich? The criteria are as follows… The tomato slice must exceed or be in proportion to the slice of bread and the juice, meaning you must use both hands to pick it up. Most importantly, the tomato should be so ripe that its mayonnaise-infused juice runs down both arms when sink your teeth into it.

Now that, folks, is good country eating!

*Baked Stuffed Tomatoes

8 good sized tomatoes
1/2 stick butter
1 large green onion top, chopped
1 cup ground beef
2 cups stale bread, softened in milk
1 egg, beaten
Salt and pepper
Parmesan cheese

Preheat oven to 350°.

Scoop the stem and inside pulp (save the pulp) from the tomatoes and turn upside down on paper towels to drain. In an iron skillet, sauté the onion top in butter until browned. Add the beef and tomato pulp to the onion and butter and cook on medium until it is not runny.

Squeeze out the milk from the stale bread, add the egg, salt and pepper to the bread and mix well. Then add to the meat and tomato mixture. Cook until it is firm. Stuff the tomato shells with this dressing and sprinkle tops with the Parmesan cheese. Bake at 350° for about 15 minutes.

Prep time: 30 minutes • Cook time: 30 minutes • Serves: 8

Creole Potatoes

2 Idaho potatoes, cubed to about 1" (or half a dozen or so new potatoes, quartered)

1 1/2 pounds smoked or summer sausage, cut to 1" pieces

1 cup fresh mushrooms, small

1 jumbo white onion, chopped coarse

Red and/or green bell pepper, sliced thin from top to bottom

2 celery sticks, cut in 1/2" pieces

Tabasco® or other hot sauce

1/4 stick of butter

Salt and pepper

Several dashes Worcestershire

Line a large bowl with heavy aluminum foil, using two or more sheets and leaving extra foil outside the bowl. Then, combine all the ingredients in the bowl, slicing the butter thin so it will mix thoroughly when cooking. Wrap the foil loosely and seal.

Grill on medium low heat for 45 minutes to 1 hour, occasionally turning and shaking to blend butter and spices.

Tracy's Tip...

This is an excellent dish to prepare for a camping trip beforehand.
Just keep cool on ice before putting on the fire grate.
Turn often. There's no clean-up, either.

Prep time: 20 minutes • Cook time: 45 minutes to 1 hour • Serves: 4 to 6

Lemon Asparagus

2 pounds fresh asparagus

1/4 cup butter

1/2 teaspoon salt

1/2 teaspoon pepper, freshly ground

1 Tablespoon grated lemon rind

1/4 cup fresh lemon juice

Snap off tough ends of asparagus; remove scales with a vegetable peeler, if desired.

Melt butter in a skillet; add asparagus, and sauté 3 minutes or until just tender. Add salt and pepper; remove from heat. Toss with lemon rind and juice.

Prep time: 10 minutes • Cook Time: 3 minutes • Serves: 4 to 6

VEGETABLES

Oriental Mushrooms

1 pound fresh mushrooms
1/2 medium onion, diced
1/2 stick butter
2 Tablespoons soy sauce
2 Tablespoons teriyaki sauce
1/2 teaspoon salt
Dash pepper
Water
2 teaspoons all purpose flour

Place onion in skillet with butter, adding soy sauce, teriyaki sauce, salt and pepper. Cook onion until it begins to brown slightly.

Mushrooms should be washed, tipped and sliced in half, from crown through stem.

Add mushrooms to butter and onions. Add 1/4 cup water. Cook on high, stirring and adding a little water when necessary (1/4 cup at a time), until mushrooms are dark and soft.

When the mushrooms have softened and browned, sift on the flour and stir well, making the consistency of a light gravy. Add more water if needed and cook for only a moment, stirring constantly.

Check the taste and add more teriyaki and soy sauce if necessary. There should be enough gravy for a balance between mushrooms and sauce. Serve in small bowls as a side dish.

Tracy's Tip...

Experiment: Try adding a little white cooking wine and /or minced clove of garlic. When served with fish, though, avoid garlic.

Prep time: 25 to 30 minutes • Cook time: 1 hour • Serves: 4 to 6

Black Eyed Peas

1 pound fresh shelled (or 1 pound package dried) black-eyed peas

Water

5 whole black peppercorns

1 bay leaf

1 medium onion, peeled and quartered

1 jalapeno pepper, halved

1 ham hock

1 small bunch curly or flat-leaf parsley

4 cloves garlic, peeled

Salt and pepper

Wash the peas in a colander and rinse under cool running water. Put in a medium stockpot and cover with about 2 inches of water. Add the peppercorns, bay leaf, onion, jalapeno pepper, ham hock, whole parsley and garlic. Add salt and pepper to taste.

Cover and bring to just below boiling over a medium-high heat. Uncover and reduce the heat, simmering until the peas are tender when bitten. Fresh peas should be checked after about 20 minutes; dried peas will take about twice as long, or longer, depending on their age. Don't stir while cooking because they will break down.

Drain peas and serve with a good topping of Chow-Chow (page 180). Or, you can serve them in their own liquor in individual bowls like a soup, with the ham hock shredded and the garlic and jalapeno thrown in.

Prep time: 10 minutes   •   Cook Time: 30 minutes to 1 hour   •   Serves: 6

Cheddar Garlic Cheese Grits

1 cup cooked grits

4 oz. garlic cheese, grated

2 cups sharp cheddar cheese, grated

2 eggs, beaten

1/4 teaspoon garlic powder

1/2 teaspoon Tabasco®

Cooking spray

Preheat oven to 350°.

Cook grits according to package directions. While they are hot, stir in both cheeses, mixing until well combined. Add the eggs, garlic powder and Tabasco® and mix well.

Coat a baking dish with cooking spray and transfer grits mixture to it. Bake 35 minutes at 350°.

Prep time: 10 minutes • Cook Time: 45 minutes • Serves: 2

Spinach Stuffed Squash

4 yellow crookneck squash

1/2 cup butter, melted

Salt and pepper

Grated Parmesan cheese

For the spinach stuffing:

1/2 cup onion, chopped

2 packages (10 oz.) frozen chopped
spinach, cooked and drained

1 teaspoon salt

1 cup sour cream

2 teaspoons red wine vinegar

1/4 cup bread crumbs

Preheat oven to 350°.

Cook whole squash in boiling, salted water for about 10 minutes or until tender. Very carefully cut into halves, top to bottom, and scoop out seeds, making a little boat. Sprinkle each shell with a little of the melted butter, salt and pepper and Parmesan cheese.

For the stuffing, sauté the onion in most of the remaining butter (not all) until tender. Add spinach, salt, sour cream and vinegar and blend well. Stuff each squash shell with the spinach mixture. Sprinkle each again with more Parmesan cheese and the bread crumbs and brush with the remaining melted butter. Put in a shallow baking dish and bake in a preheated oven at 350° for about 15 minutes.

Prep time: 20 minutes • Cook Time: 30 minutes • Serves: 6 to 8

Dixie Relish

1 pint sweet red peppers, chopped

1 quart cabbage, chopped

1 pint sweet green peppers

1 pint onions, chopped

2 hot peppers

5 Tablespoons salt

4 Tablespoons mustard seed

2 Tablespoons celery seed

1/2 cup sugar

1 quart white vinegar

Mix vegetables together and cover with salt. Let stand overnight in the refrigerator.

Drain well, put in a big pot, add spices, sugar and vinegar. Pack into sterilized canning jars to within about 1/2" of the top and cap tightly. Then, place in a big boiler and boil for 5 minutes.

Prep time: 30 minutes • Marinate: overnight • Cook time: 20 minutes • Yields: 5 pints canned relish

Hot Damn Roasted Red Peppers

3 large red peppers

2 Tablespoons extra virgin olive oil

1/4 teaspoon rosemary

1/4 teaspoon basil

1/4 teaspoon garlic powder

Slice two or three large red peppers in about 1" strips lengthwise, remove seeds and ribs.

Place on grill (or in oven) inside up. Roast until the skin begins to burn (in oven, 20 minutes on 400°). Remove and seal in paper bag for 15 minutes. Take out and peel off skin.

Splash with extra virgin olive oil and sprinkle herbs over top. Serve as an appetizer or side vegetable with red meat.

Prep time: 15 minutes   •   Cook Time: 45 minutes   •   Serves: 6 to 8

Spiced Baked Louisiana Yams

4 medium yams, cooked and peeled

1/4 teaspoon ginger

1/4 cup brown sugar

1/3 cup butter, melted

1/2 teaspoon nutmeg

2 teaspoons dark rum

Preheat oven to 350°.

Arrange yams in a shallow baking dish. Combine other ingredients and mix well. Pour over the yams and bake at 350° for 30 minutes.

Prep time: 35 minutes • Cook time: 30 minutes • Serves: 4

Orange Candied Yams

6 medium yams

1 cup orange juice

1/4 cup butter

1/2 teaspoon salt

1 cup water

1 cup sugar

1/2 teaspoon grated orange rind

Preheat oven to 350°.

Peel and slice the uncooked yams in about 1/4" round slices and arrange in a buttered baking dish. Combine the other ingredients into a syrup and pour over the yams. Cover and bake at 350° until tender, spoon-basting with the syrup about every 10 minutes. Then uncover and bake for another 10 minutes, letting the tops brown.

Tracy's Tip...

For an extra treat, add a layer of marshmallows and let brown just before removing from the oven.

Prep time: 10 minutes • Cook Time: 20 minutes • Serves: 6 to 8

String Bean's Casserole

2 cans French cut green beans, drained

1 medium white onion, cut into thin rings

6 strips bacon, fried and crumbled

6 teaspoons bacon drippings

6 teaspoons sugar

4 teaspoons apple cider vinegar

1 teaspoon salt

1/2 teaspoon pepper

Preheat oven to 350°.

Layer the beans, then the onion rings then crumbled bacon in a casserole dish. Combine the remaining 5 ingredients over medium heat then pour mixture over the completed casserole. Cover tightly with foil and refrigerate overnight. Uncover and bake at 350° for 1 hour.

Tracy's Tip...

Makes a great casserole dish when you have to contribute to a covered dish supper. Just cover with foil and re-heat.

Prep time: 20 to 25 minutes • Marinate: overnight • Cook time: 1 hour • Serves: 4

My Favorite Baked Bean Recipe

1 jar (16 oz.) baked beans

1 large yellow onion, diced

1/2 cup dark Kayro syrup

1/3 cup ketchup

1 Tablespoon Worcestershire

1 teaspoon dry mustard

3 bacon strips

Preheat oven to 350°.

Mix ingredients (except bacon) well, place in a baking crock or Dutch oven and cover with the bacon strips. Bake at 350° for about an hour.

Prep time: 5 minutes • Cook Time: 1 hour • Serves: 4

VEGETABLES

Veggie Lasagna

6 lasagna noodles, cooked

15 oz. frozen, chopped spinach

1/2 cup chopped onion

1 teaspoon oil

1 cup carrots, grated

2 cups fresh mushrooms, sliced

1 can (15 oz.) tomato sauce

1 can (6 oz.) tomato paste

1/2 cup pitted ripe olives, drained and chopped

1 1/2 teaspoon dried oregano

2 cups cottage cheese, strained

1 pound Monterey Jack cheese, sliced

1/4 cup Parmesan cheese, grated

Preheat oven to 375°.

Prepare spinach according to package directions. Drain. Meanwhile, sauté onions in oil until soft. Add carrots and mushrooms; cook until crisp-tender. Stir in tomato sauce, tomato paste, olives and oregano. Butter or grease a 13x9x2" casserole or pan. Layer in one-half each of noodles, cottage cheese, spinach, sauce mixture, and 1/2 of the cheese slices. Repeat. Sprinkle with Parmesan cheese and bake for 30 minutes.

Prep time: 30 minutes • Cook time: 30 minutes • Serves: 8

Chow Chow

6 pounds green tomatoes, chopped

5 green bell peppers, chopped

4 large onions, chopped

1 1/2 Tablespoons salt

3 hot peppers, chopped

16 oz. white vinegar

1/4 teaspoon cloves

1 Tablespoon allspice

3 bay leaves

1 1/2 Tablespoons dry mustard

1/2 cup sugar

1/4 cup horseradish

In a food processor mix the tomatoes, bell peppers and onions. Cover with the salt and let it stand overnight in the refrigerator.

Drain really well; I even sometimes squeeze the moisture out using a colander. Add the hot peppers, vinegar, spices (tied in a cheese cloth bag) and sugar. Boil slowly for about 15 to 20 minutes. Remove the spices. Add the horseradish, stirring to combine. Pack into sterilized canning jars to within 1/2" of the top and cap tightly. Then, place in a big boiler and boil for 5 minutes. Goes great on black-eyed peas (page 170).

Prep time: 30 minutes • Marinate: overnight • Cook time: 30 minutes • Serves: 12

VEGETABLES

Desserts

The Watermelon Crawl

One of my favorite songs I've recorded is "Watermelon Crawl". It's a fun, summertime tune my fans seem to love singing along with. The song is about a fictitious place in Georgia where the entire town has turned out for the annual watermelon festival. It is one of those events where watermelon is served up in every conceivable fashion, including wine…

I was driving thru Georgia in late July
On a day hot enough to make the Devil sigh
I saw a homemade sign written in red
Rind County Watermelon Festival Ahead
Well, I wasn't in a hurry so I slowed down
Took a two lane road to a one horse town
There was a party going on when I got there
I heard a welcome speech from a small town mayor

He said we got a hundred gallons of sweet red wine
Made from the biggest watermelons on the vine
Help yourself to some but obey the law
If you drink don't drive do the watermelon crawl

If you live in the South then you know that eating ice cold watermelon ranks right up there with homemade lemonade as a Fourth of July tradition. Watermelon is as much a part of Fourth of July backyard cookouts as burgers, hot dogs, baked beans and slaw.

I don't advise trying to make wine from watermelon because there are so many other ways to enjoy this summertime treat. I know this for a fact since many of my fans have come to our shows to share their favorite watermelon dessert recipes. What these creative cooks come up with will blow your mind.

Have you ever had watermelon gelatin? Some of the other delicious, but strange watermelon treats we've had include Popsicles, pies, cakes and sherbet. One lady even brought us a watermelon mousse. Now that's something you just don't find everywhere!

* Watermelon Cubes

This is an easy recipe that's great to do with the kids for a cold summertime treat!

1 watermelon

Cut watermelon into medium sized, workable pieces. Remove the seeds and the rind and puree the watermelon in a food processor or blender. Once smooth, pour the puree into ice cube trays and freeze.

Tracy's Tip...

You can turn these into Watermelon Pops by sticking a popsicle stick in each cube while freezing... then you'll be able to enjoy these on the go.

Prep time: 10 minutes • Cook time: Freezing • Serves: 4 to 8

Butterscotch Brownies

2 1/2 cups all purpose flour

1 teaspoon baking powder

1/2 teaspoon salt

1 cup butter, softened

1 3/4 cup brown sugar, packed

1 Tablespoon vanilla extract

2 eggs

1 2/3 cup (11 oz. pkg) Nestle® Tollhouse Butterscotch morsels, divided

1 cup chopped nuts (optional)

Preheat oven to 350°.

Combine flour, baking powder and salt in medium bowl. Beat butter, brown sugar and vanilla extract in large mixing bowl until creamy. Beat in eggs. Gradually add in flour mixture, the butterscotch morsels and nuts. Spread into ungreased 13x9" baking pan. Sprinkle with remaining morsels.

Bake 30 to 40 minutes or until a wooden toothpick inserted in center comes out clean.

Prep time: 15 minutes • Cook time: 40 minutes • Yield: 4 dozen

Apple Coffee Cake

1 package dry yeast

2 teaspoons warm water

2 teaspoons sugar

1 egg, slightly beaten

1/2 cup milk, scalded and cooled

1/2 teaspoon salt

1/2 cup butter

2 cups sifted flour

6 to 8 apples, pared and sliced

For the topping:

3/4 cup sugar

1 teaspoon cinnamon

1/4 cup butter

Dissolve yeast in water; add sugar, egg, milk and salt. Cut butter into flour as for a pie crust. Add yeast mixture, beat thoroughly. Spread dough into buttered jelly roll pan 15x10", cover and let rise until doubled in bulk (45-60 minutes). Top with apples in rows over dough.

Topping:
Preheat oven to 375°.

Mix sugar and cinnamon and sprinkle over apples. Dot with butter and bake at 375° for 25 minutes. Best when served warm. Makes two dozen slices.

Prep time: 15 minutes • Cook Time: 1 1/2 hours • Serves: 12 to18

Candy Bar Brownies

4 large eggs, lightly beaten

2 cups sugar

3/4 cups butter, melted

2 teaspoons vanilla

1 1/2 cup all purpose flour

1/2 teaspoon baking powder

1/4 teaspoon salt

1/3 cup cocoa

4 (2.07 oz.) chocolate-coated caramel-peanut nougat bars, coarsely chopped

3 (1.55 oz.) milk chocolate bars, finely chopped

Preheat oven to 350°.

Combine eggs, sugar, butter, and vanilla extract in a large bowl. In a separate bowl, combine flour, baking powder, salt and cocoa; stir into sugar mixture. Fold in chopped nougat bars. Spoon into a greased and floured 13x9x2" pan. Sprinkle with chopped milk chocolate bars. Bake at 350° for 30 to 35 minutes. Cool. Cut into squares and serve.

Prep time: 15 minutes • Cook time: 30 to 35 minutes • Yield: 2 1/2 dozen

Tracy's Treat

Graham crackers

1 cup butter

1/2 cup sugar

Pecan pieces

Preheat oven to 350°.

Break graham crackers into pieces and put in bottom of 13x9" baking dish. Combine butter and sugar, bring to a boil, and boil for 3 minutes, stirring constantly. Pour over graham crackers, sprinkle with pecan pieces to cover. Bake at 350° for 12 minutes; remove, allow to partially cool (until frosting is kind of setting up), then remove to foil to cool completely.

Prep time: 10 minutes • Cook Time: 15 minutes • Yield: 12 servings

Fresh Apple Cake

3 cups Granny Smith apples, peeled and sliced into small wedges

2 cups sugar

1 1/2 cups oil

2 eggs

2 teaspoons vanilla

1 cup pecans, chopped

2 1/2 cups flour

1 1/2 teaspoons baking soda

1/2 teaspoon salt

1/2 teaspoon ground cinnamon

For the topping:

1 cup dark brown sugar

1/2 stick butter

1 1/2 Tablespoons corn starch

3/4 cup water

Preheat oven to 300°.

Mix apples, sugar, oil, eggs and vanilla; sift in dry ingredients (except nuts), blend well, then add nuts. Bake in 9x13" pan 1 hour at 300°.

Topping :
Mix ingredients in sauce pan, cook over medium heat till thick. Pour over cake and serve.

Prep time: 20 minutes   •   Cook time: 1 hour   •   Serves: 12

Lemonade Cake

1 package lemon Jell-O®

1 cup water

1 box yellow cake mix

3/4 cup vegetable oil

4 eggs

For the icing:

1 cup confectioner's sugar

1 can (6 oz.) frozen lemonade, thawed

Preheat oven to 350°.

Dissolve Jell-O® in 1 cup hot water and let cool. Add remaining ingredients to cooled Jell-O® and bake in ungreased bundt pan at 350° for 45 minutes.

Icing:
Mix and pour over cooled cake.

Prep time: 10 minutes • Cook Time: 45 minutes • Serves: 12

Florida Cake

1 package yellow cake mix

2/3 cup vegetable oil

2 eggs

1 can (10 oz.) mandarin oranges, undrained

For the frosting:

1 large tub Cool Whip®

1 package vanilla pudding

1 cup crushed pineapple

Preheat oven to 350°.

Combine cake mix, oil and eggs, beat 4 minutes. Fold in mandarin oranges and juice. Pour into 9x12" pan and bake 25 minutes at 350°.

Frosting:
Combine ingredients and frost cooled cake. Keep cake refrigerated till ready to serve.

Prep time: 10 minutes • Cook time: 25 minutes • Serves: 12

Sinful Southern Brownies

1/2 cup melted Crisco® shortening

2 eggs

1 cup sugar

1 teaspoon baking powder

1/2 teaspoon salt

1/2 cup flour

1/4 cup + 1 Tablespoon Hershey's® Coco

1 teaspoon vanilla

1 cup chopped nuts (optional)

Preheat oven to 325°.

   Melt shortening over medium heat. Set aside to cool. Beat eggs in large mixing bowl, sift dry ingredients (except nuts) into eggs, stir well. Pour cooled shortening into mixture and blend, add vanilla and nuts. Bake in shallow 10x10" pan for 25 to 30 minutes at 325°.

Prep time: 20 minutes   •   Cook Time: 30 minutes   •   Serves: 8

Plum Cake

3 eggs

2 cups sugar

1 cup vegetable oil

2 jars baby food plum desserts

2 cups self-rising flour

1 Tablespoon cinnamon

1 Tablespoon allspice

1 Tablespoon nutmeg

1 Tablespoon ground cloves

1 cup chopped pecans

In large bowl, beat eggs, add sugar, oil and plums. Mix well. Sift flour and then add spices and nuts. Pour into 9x12" baking dish. Place in cold oven, turn heat to 300° and cook for 1 1/2 hours.

Prep time: 20 minutes • Cook time: 1 1/2 hours • Serves: 10

Chocolate Pie

1/2 stick butter

1 1/2 cups sugar

3 Tablespoons cocoa

1/2 cup pecans

2 eggs, slightly beaten

1 teaspoon vanilla

1 teaspoon flour

1/2 cup evaporated milk

1 9" piecrust, unbaked

Preheat oven to 400°.

Melt the butter in a large bowl. Add the next 7 ingredients, mixing thoroughly. Pour the mixture into the piecrust. Bake for 10 minutes at 400°. Reduce oven temperature to 325° and bake for an additional 30 minutes.

Prep time: 20 minutes • Cook Time: 40 minutes • Serves: 8

Coffee Ice Cream Crunch

1 cup flour, sifted

1/4 cup oatmeal

1/4 cup brown sugar

1/2 cup butter

1/2 cup pecans, chopped

1 jar (12 oz.) caramel sauce

1 quart coffee (or chocolate) ice cream

Preheat oven to 400°.

Combine oatmeal, flour and brown sugar. Cut in the butter until crumbly. Stir in the nuts. Put mixture in to a 13x9" pan and bake at 400° for 15 minutes. Remove and stir while still hot to crumble, then let cool completely. Spread half the crumbs in to a 9x9" pan. Drizzle about half of the caramel over the crumbs in the bottom of the pan. Stir the ice cream to soften and spoon into pan. Drizzle with the remaining caramel and sprinkle with the remaining crumbs. Freeze until ice cream is hard again.

Prep time: 15 minutes • Cook time: 15 minutes • Freeze time: 45 minutes • Serves: 8

Sweet Pecan Bites

2 cups all purpose flour

1/2 cup sugar

1/8 teaspoon salt

1 1/4 cups butter, divided

1 cup brown sugar, firmly packed

1 cup light corn syrup

4 large eggs, lightly beaten

2 1/2 cups pecans, finely chopped

1 teaspoon vanilla extract

Preheat oven to 350°.

Combine the flour, sugar and salt in a large bowl, and cut in 3/4 cup butter with a pastry blender until the mixture resembles very fine crumbs. Press the mixture into a greased 13x9" pan. Bake at 350° for 17 to 20 minutes, or until lightly browned.

While crust is baking, combine the brown sugar, corn syrup and 1/2 cup butter in a saucepan. Bring to a boil over medium heat, stirring gently. Remove from the heat. Stir 1/4 of the hot mixture into the beaten eggs, and then pour this mixture in to the remaining hot mixture. Add in the pecans and vanilla, stirring to combine. Pour the filling over the crust.

Bake for 35 minutes, or until set. Cool completely in the pan on a wire rack. Cut into bite size pieces.

Prep time: 5 minutes • Cook Time: 1 hour • Yields: 30 pieces

About Tracy

This is Tracy...

*T*racy Byrd knows more about country music legends Hank Williams, Bob Wills and Jimmie Rodgers than most of his talented peers. Admittedly, he is a student of traditional country music and he sings the real thing… the traditional sound that echoes in the honky-tonks of his native southeast Texas home.

Byrd was born and raised in the rural piney woods near Beaumont and grew up listening to his parent's extensive country music record collection. In his early 20s, Byrd visited a novelty recording studio at a local mall and sang karaoke-style to the track of "Your Cheatin' Heart." The store owner was so impressed she signed him up for an amateur talent show where the inexperienced and stage-shy Byrd sang "Weary Blues" and "Folsom Prison Blues" in front of an audience. A standing ovation was all it took for Byrd to recognize his calling.

"They had to drag me onstage," Byrd says jokingly, "Two songs later, they had to drag me off, because I fell in love with it that quick." From then on, he concentrated almost exclusively on his new chosen career, performing traditional country music five nights a week in the bars of Beaumont. The hard work paid off and he scored a major recording contract just a few years later in 1992.

For over a decade now, Tracy Byrd has enjoyed the kind of career that most only dream about. He's achieved longevity in today's business of 'here today, gone tomorrow' and 'one hit wonder' syndromes. He consistently cuts records fans love, such as the up-tempo sing-a-longs "Watermelon Crawl" and "I'm From The Country," to his recent "Ten Rounds With Jose Cuervo" and "Drinkin' Bone." Those goodhearted tunes are balanced with love songs, like his signature song "The Keeper Of the Stars." It won the Academy of Country Music's Song of the Year in 1995 and was the fifth biggest selling piece of sheet music, trailing themes from *The Lion King*, *Forest Gump* and *Pocahontas*. It remains a wedding favorite today.

In his personal time or on home ground, Byrd relaxes with a golf club, fishing rod or bow. To say that this multi-platinum recording artist loves the outdoors doesn't come close to conveying the actual obsession he has with fishing and hunting.

"I've always loved to fish and hunt," he proclaims. "It's my No. 1 passion next to family and music," says Byrd, who aspired to become a professional bass angler and host his own outdoor TV show even before his music career took off.

Byrd's love of the outdoors was passed onto him honestly by his grandmother, Mavis Vaughn, whom he affectionately called NaNa.

"NaNa started me fishing when I was 3 or 4 years old and she took me hunting when I got a little older," he says. "She was never your average grandmother type. She bought me my first shotgun when I was six years old. I deer hunted with her, did a little bit of duck hunting and quite a bit of small game hunting, too.

"A few years back, I took her on a turkey shoot at King Ranch in South Texas," he adds. "She'd probably never seen a wild turkey before, but NaNa killed herself a big tom. We've got the whole thing on film. It was awesome!"

"One of my peers once told me I was a 'recreatin' son of a gun' and I thought that was a pretty good description of me. I love the outdoors and appreciate the positive issues of wildlife management and I hope I pass every bit of it on to my kids."

Tracy Byrd is also known as a nice guy who gives back to his community.

"I want to do well with what I've been given. My Homecoming Weekend is my vehicle to do that."

The annual Tracy Byrd Homecoming Weekend event is a fundraiser full of fishing, golf and music. His longtime support and contributions to his hometown are evidenced by the Tracy Byrd Hyperbaric Medicine and Wound Care Center at Christus St. Elizabeth Hospital. The facility is the only one of its kind in southeast Texas that greatly improves the quality of life for brain-injured children.

Beaumont's native son is the full star package, loaded with talent and a heart as big as his state. His rich, baritone voice passionately delivers the plain-spoken message of country music. And, he loves to fish and hunt, too.

Index

Tracy's Tip...

Remember to always have fun in the kitchen!